Violent and Aggressive Youth

Practical Skills for Counselors
Jeffrey A. Kottler, Series Editor

Fred Bemak • Susan Keys

Violent and Aggressive Youth

*Intervention and Prevention
Strategies for Changing Times*

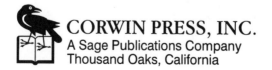

CORWIN PRESS, INC.
A Sage Publications Company
Thousand Oaks, California

For information:

Corwin Press, Inc.
A Sage Publications Company
2455 Teller Road
Thousand Oaks, California 91320
E-mail: order@corwinpress.com

SAGE Publications Ltd.
6 Bonhill Street
London EC2A 4PU
United Kingdom

SAGE Publications India Pvt. Ltd.
M-32 Market
Greater Kailash I
New Delhi 110 048 India

Printed in the United States of America

Library of Congress Cataloging-in-Publication Data

Bemak, Fred.
    Violent and aggressive youth: Intervention and prevention strategies for changing times / Fred Bemak, Susan Keys.
        p. cm. — (Practical skills for counselors series)
    Includes bibliographical references and index.
    ISBN 0-8039-6825-6 (cloth: alk. paper)
    ISBN 0-8039-6826-4 (pbk: alk. paper)
    1. School violence—United States—Prevention. 2. Juvenile delinquency—United States—Prevention. I. Keys, Susan. II. Title.
III. Series: Practical skills for counselors
    LB3013.3 .B45 1999
    371.7′8—dc21
                                                            99-6355

This book is printed on acid-free paper.

00 01 02 03 04 05 06 10 9 8 7 6 5 4 3 2 1

Production Editor: S. Marlene Head
Editorial Assistant: Kristen L. Gibson
Typesetter: Rebecca Evans
Cover Designer: Michelle Lee

Contents

Preface

This book is designed for school counselors, teachers, and administrators who are on the front line of facing the growing violence in today's schools. Violence is one of the most complex and difficult student problems we face in public education. It interferes with students' academic performance, career options, and personal and social growth, and it threatens the very safety of students and faculty. The book provides school counselors and other staff with practical principles and guidelines for understanding and providing effective interventions and developing prevention models to deal with the aggressive student.

Unique Features

Most professionals who work in schools are not trained to deal with violence. At the same time, incidents of violence are growing dramatically in urban, suburban, and rural schools. This book outlines national trends, describes what places someone at risk of violent and aggressive behavior, and presents new prevention and intervention strategies focused specifically on violence. The content of the book is based on the literature, pilot and implementation projects, consultations by the two authors with schools throughout the United States, and interviews and discussions with numerous colleagues working in schools.

Contents of the Book

The first chapter provides an overview of the literature on school violence as a foundation for understanding the problem. In this chapter, we examine the pervasiveness of the problem, offer some caution in interpreting these findings, and discuss the effects of violence. The chapter also discusses general themes related to counselors, teachers, administrators, and students in relationship to aggression.

Chapter 2 moves beyond incidents and trends to explain who aggressive youth are. An examination of individual factors, peer influence, and family relationships is presented, as well as a discussion of factors of school violence that originate and are linked directly to schools and associated communities. Chapter 2 also looks at violence prevention within schools, larger systems, families, peer groups, and communities.

The third chapter describes individually focused interventions with violent youth. Counselor self-awareness, intervention goals, establishment of trust with aggressive youth, and suggestions for achieving positive outcomes are presented.

Chapter 4 offers specific intervention principles for work with both individuals and groups. This chapter provides innovative suggestions in each of these areas.

The fifth chapter discusses how to institute collaborative efforts in designing and implementing violence prevention programs. Systemic issues, potential partners, and community participation are discussed. The chapter also describes specific skills for facilitating collaborative partnerships and group problem solving.

The sixth chapter discusses the importance of knowing ourselves as a means to become truly effective in reducing school violence. Self-awareness and the difficulty of not judging the aggressive child are discussed. The chapter continues to present recommendations for issues such as self-disclosure, modeling, self-monitoring, and debriefing.

The afterword offers a concluding thought from the authors to people working in this field.

Please note that all names of schools and students in this book are fictitious.

Acknowledgments

I, Fred Bemak, cannot begin to express my gratitude and appreciation to my lovely and special wife, Rita Chi-Ying Chung, for her gracious and loving support and patience as I immersed myself in the work and commitment necessary to write this book. In addition, for my ever-present teachers—my parents Walter and Ruth Bemak, who provided the wonderful childhood that gave me the balance and inner strength to work with children and adolescents, and my children, Amber and Lani Bemak, who provide me with a source of belonging and connectedness to myself and the world in ways that make life meaningful—my unending gratitude and love. And of course, to my coauthor and one of my favorite colleagues, Susan, with whom I have been through many a difficult workday and tackled major projects like this book, but who still comes out laughing . . . thank you.

I, Susan Keys, realize that the art of putting words on paper in a meaningful way—"writing"—requires a considerable amount of time. My family—John, Erin, and Caitlin—could not have been more supportive and understanding, even when my commitment to complete this book meant much less time for them. My colleague and coauthor, Fred, brought considerable talent and a healthy dose of humor to our writing task. Fred, we did it! But then, you never doubted that we would.

About the Authors

Fred Bemak is Professor of Counselor Education and Section Head of Wellness and Human Services at Ohio State University.

Susan Keys is an Assistant Professor and Chair of the Department of Counseling and Human Services at Johns Hopkins University.

Both authors have done extensive national work in schools focusing on innovative strategies to work with at-risk youth, including the development and implementation of aggression and violence prevention and intervention programs.

1

Danger Zones in Schools

Many schools in the United States today are like minefields in a war zone. No one is quite sure when the next explosion or episode of violent behavior is going to occur, yet when it does, the effects can be traumatic and devastating. To ensure the safety of students and faculty, schools are implementing more stringent policies related to student behavior in general, and possession of weapons at school in particular. In many school systems, carrying a weapon results in out-of-school suspension or expulsion. This rule is enforced regardless of the type of weapon, intent, or student age. Recently, when we were meeting with an elementary school principal, the principal left our meeting after a knock at the door. Later, we discovered that she had been summoned to initiate suspension procedures for a first-grade student who had brought a small knife to school to cut his apple at lunchtime. Although it could be argued that the intent and the age of the student would require a much more lenient response, this incident represents how serious today's schools are about protecting students and school staff from aggression or violence.

How pervasive is the problem of violence and aggression in schools today, and how does working and learning in a danger zone affect teachers and students? This first chapter responds to these fundamental questions and provides an overview of key issues. Subsequent chapters address what school counselors can do to help their schools preserve a safe learning environment. Specifically, Chapter 2 looks more closely at the factors in a student's life that may contribute to violent and aggressive behavior, and Chapter 3 offers concrete advice and guiding principles for using many of the skills that counselors already have that apply to interventions with violent and aggressive students. Chapter 4 addresses innovative interventions and group work with this population, whereas Chapter 5 provides suggestions for collaborative partnerships focusing on prevention that reach beyond the school to families and the broader community. Chapter 6 cautions counselors about personal issues that might interfere with professional judgment when working with violent and aggressive youth.

Beware, Danger Ahead

One needs only to keep abreast of daily news headlines to realize that the potential for violence in schools is very real and frightening. When considering violence and aggression in schools, it has been suggested that there are two types of schools: those that have had a significant violent incident, and those that will. Schools, once felt to be a safe haven for students, can no longer promise that the violence occurring in society and neighborhood communities will not permeate their walls. Even if schools do not encounter extreme incidents, they must cope daily with a variety of student behaviors that jeopardize a safe school climate.

Are Fears Justified?

As school personnel, there is a context for the intervention and prevention programs that we develop to work with violent youth. We contend that it is important to understand the trends and generalized incidents of violence within our own schools, districts, and states, as well as within our nation, before we race off and develop strategies to reduce aggression within our schools and districts. This bigger picture gives us a far better foundation to understand the problem, knowing what violent behaviors are increasing or decreasing, what the trends and patterns are, and where the pockets of problem areas are. This information helps us better understand how our experience fits into the context of the school and how we can be more effective at addressing this problem.

Many of you work in schools where violent and aggressive behavior has become a normal part of the daily milieu. To give you a more complete larger picture about how your school or district fits into the national picture, we point to a 1998 review by the federal government examining the perceptions of principals about crime and violence as a serious problem in public schools. More than half indicated that their school experienced at least one crime incident in the 1996-1997 school year, and 1 in 10 reported at least one serious violent crime. As a group, they reported about 4,000 incidents of rape or other type of sexual battery, 11,000 incidents of physical attacks or fights in which weapons were used, about 190,000 fights or physical attacks not involving weapons, 115,000 thefts, and 98,000 incidents of vandalism. All crimes that occurred at school and were reported to the police or other law enforcement representatives—including incidents that took place in school buildings, on school grounds, on school buses, and at school-sponsored events or activities, but not officially on school grounds—are included in these figures. Of the principals surveyed, 21% ranked conflict among students as a serious or moderate problem in their school. Incidents that occurred in your schools are probably included in these figures. These numbers might also be an underrepresentation of what actually occurs in schools. Your experience working in schools may also be consistent with these figures. Remember, these numbers included only acts that resulted in a report to the police. We would suspect that additional acts occurred but were not deemed serious enough to report to the police. (Readers who would like more information about the results of this national survey should contact the National Center for Education Statistics and ask for publication #98-030).

When students are asked to report about their own behavior, they also indicate a serious concern about violence or the potential for violence in schools. A national study found that almost 40% of teenage students between the ages of 12 and 21 had engaged in at least one physical fight in the year preceding the Center's survey; for teens aged 14 to 17, this number was slightly more than one in four. Rates were slightly higher, at one in two, for black, non-Hispanic teens in this age group. Younger teens, 12 to 13 years of age, had similar rates of about one in two having fights during the preceding year. This information is important for school personnel to know because it provides a baseline for where some of the trouble spots are related to school violence.

Youths were asked on how many days during the past month they had carried a weapon, such as a gun, knife, or club. Youths who had carried a weapon were then asked to identify the kind of weapon they had carried most frequently. Seventeen percent of teens 14 to 17 years of age said they carried a weapon, compared to more than 1 out of 10 of those aged 12 to 13. For more than half of the students aged 12 to 21, knives were the weapon most frequently carried, followed by almost one fourth who carried firearms, and slightly more than one tenth who carried clubs. Trying to get a handle on the levels of violence in schools, another study asked students in Grades 7 to 12 about their perceptions of violence in school. The numbers are alarming. Almost two thirds reported being verbally insulted; more than one third had something stolen; and more than one third of the students had been pushed, shoved, or grabbed. More than one in four students had been threatened, whereas one in five students had been kicked, bitten, or hit with a fist while in school. Again, these figures are important for you as a teacher, counselor, or administrator in schools to know, because this is what is going on in our environments and provides us with a general rule of thumb when working with youth.

Some states have grown increasingly concerned about violence within the state's own schools. To better understand these national trends, and to see if these trends were consistent with what was going on statewide, many states have begun to collect information that was more specific to them. For example, the Virginia Department of Education wanted to know more about violence, drug possession, weapon violations, and other high-risk behaviors in their schools. They found that the highest rates of fighting were among younger teens in Grades 8, 9, and 10, and that the students became more violent as they were involved in more incidents of serious assaults that required professional medical attention. They also found increased drug possession in Grades 9 to 12 that seemed to relate to more violations for having weapons, which, most of the time, was a knife. South Carolina found similar results, with sharp increases in school crime that included disturbances in school, drug and narcotics violations, possession of pagers, weapons offenses, aggravated assaults, larceny/thefts, vandalism/destruction of property, burglary/breaking and entering, threatening school officials or their family members, and liquor violations—which accounted for nearly 97% of the crimes. It might be helpful to you to look up relevant statistics in your state as well.

These figures may be representative of other states as well and probably confirm what many of you already know and experience from working in schools. We believe that it is important for you to have an understanding of these overall trends so that you can make sense of what you do to address violence in your schools and know where some of the major problems rest. Many of you have witnessed student fights, classroom disruptions, and other intimidating interpersonal behavior. Some of you have intervened directly to stop such behavior. At one time or another, most of you in your professional role have helped both victims and perpetrators in the aftermath of a violent or aggressive episode. These figures only accentuate what you already know and experience, unfortunately demonstrate that you are not alone with these problems, and assist you in figuring out how your school fits into the larger picture.

A Word of Caution

In reading reports about violence in your schools or looking at districtwide or even some of the national or state figures that are cited above, we urge you to look at these with caution. Although these statistics may confirm your personal experience about the dangerous nature of some of today's schools, it is important to look at these reports with a critical eye.

Sometimes, different studies may collect different types of information in different ways. This makes it difficult to compare incidents of violence. For example, one report in your school might be based on documentation of incidents of certain kinds of behavior so that your school could record each time a specific type of violent behavior occurred. This could be each time a serious fight occurs, with serious defined as "one or more participants sought medical treatment." This would be consistent with the inner-city high school that the authors visited where the principal offhandedly commented, "If there isn't blood, it isn't important." Other reports may rely on self-reports by victims—for example, how many times a student was pushed, shoved, hit, intimidated, and so on; whereas still other reports may ask students, administrators, or teachers to provide their opinions about school violence. When reading and trying to understand this information, it is important for you to know on what the report is based, especially given the strong and diverse opinions about what constitutes violence.

These different definitions of what is a "violent incident" may make it difficult to compare information and get a firm grip on what is going on in your school or district. For example, you may read a report that says, "Schools report violent incidents decrease during the previous school year." Closer scrutiny of the report might indicate that the definition of a "violent incident" included only altercations involving a weapon. Such a definition probably fails to incorporate incidents you might characterize as violent.

It is also important for you to understand the potential for population differences in the results you are reading. For example, one national report cited in this chapter included adolescents who were classified as out of school. As you know, this is an important subpopulation when studying high-risk behavior. When youths who were in school were compared with out-of-school youths, as you might expect, those who had left school early had higher rates of high-risk behavior than did those who had remained in school. Including this subgroup in the report would automatically account for higher percentages of violent behavior. Yet yours and other schools generally include only youths who are currently enrolled in the educational system.

One problem with school violence surveys is that they typically include only questions that relate exclusively to violence. Some experts have observed that schools rarely ask students to compare school violence with other pressing worries or concerns, such as getting good grades, having friends, getting along with parents, and so on. If school violence surveys did collect this type of information, schools might discover that students are concerned not only about violence, but also about many associated issues that relate to violence within the school environment. This points to an important issue about how we may be able to link school violence with many other associated issues facing students when conducting needs assessments. Look again at what information you are gathering. Does your needs assessment survey include items about school safety as well as other personal, interpersonal, and academic needs? Is school safety a concern for your students? How does this compare with other high-ranked needs? If you have not included items about school safety in your survey, you might consider including such items in the future. When working with counselors to design needs assessment instruments, we recommend that counselors ask such questions as, "Do you worry *too much* about . . .?" as opposed to "Do you worry about . . .?" This emphasis on "worry *too much*" seems to better discriminate needs of real concern from worries that are more typical.

Sometimes, the incidents of violence appear to increase over time when, in fact, incidents may have remained constant. This could occur for a number of reasons. Your school or district may be improving their reporting procedures or changing these procedures altogether. The instruments used to collect self-report data may not be reliable. It is important that you are aware of these issues in order to accurately measure and understand the prevalence of violence in your school.

Effects of Violence

Generally, when we think of violent or aggressive behavior, we think of an act that causes physical harm. Just as powerful and sometimes less recognizable is the psychological harm that can result from a violent or aggressive act. The psychological harm that occurs in an environment plagued by violence and aggression is not to be underestimated. As counselors, teachers, and administrators, you have probably seen these effects all too often. Teachers who are concerned for their safety are less able to focus on teaching and student learning; students who worry about being safe are less able to concentrate and succeed academically. Many keep these fears to themselves. Normalizing fears and letting people know that they are not alone in how they feel are important functions for school counselors, teachers, and administrators.

Mrs. Washington was a new teacher in an urban school that had a reputation for having a tough student population. Shortly after beginning her new position, Mrs. Washington developed headaches and had trouble sleeping at night. Although she knew she was feeling anxious about her work environment, she felt uncomfortable saying anything about her concerns because she was new. It wasn't until the school counselors facilitated an open discussion at a faculty meeting about work-related stress in their particular school environment that Mrs. Washington realized that her colleagues shared some of her same concerns and reactions. As a result, Mrs. Washington felt some relief personally as the faculty formed a task force to look more deeply into the issue of job-related stress and steps that this school community could take to address its causes.

Posttraumatic stress disorder can result from exposure to episodes of violence even for youth and adults who are not direct victims. Maria was just such a case. Maria lives in a low-income neighborhood marked by high levels of drug-related crime and violence. She witnessed her uncle being beaten and stabbed repeatedly on the corner near her home. Maria replays the incident over and over again in her mind and worries about her own safety. She can't sleep at night because of her worries. Some days, she can't concentrate in school and even falls asleep because of the lack of sleep the night before. Maria's teachers fear she might fail if she doesn't begin to hand in more work. Some days, Maria just doesn't care. She rarely hangs out with the other kids in her neighborhood and has little interest in the fun things she used to do with her group of friends. School counselors and other personnel have an important role in helping teachers recognize kids like Maria. Images that repeat the violent episode, an inability to experience emotion, fear that the violent act may occur again, anxiety, difficulty sleeping, disinterest in school work or social activities, feelings of guilt, and difficulty paying attention are some of the aftereffects that can result from exposure to acts of violence. Once identified, the school counselor or other personnel can facilitate the appropriate referral processes, provide direct service to students like Maria and their families, and help school staff understand why students are not achieving optimally in their academic subjects.

Counselor, Teacher, and Staff Responses

Intimidation and fear are not uncommon feelings for counselors, teachers, and staff who work in schools where crime and violence prevail. In fact, these feelings may actually add to the problem. Being afraid of Maurice is a good example. He is a big 11th grader known for being aggressive. Part of his reputation is to not take "anything" from school staff. A story that has remained a school legacy was the time Maurice faced down two teachers who were reprimanding him in the hallway. Both teachers were unsettled when he scowled at them and focused his attention toward them in a threatening manner. Rumors have circulated for the past year that it wouldn't be a "good thing to mess with Maurice because he just may get you back." It is very difficult for counselors, teachers, or staff to confront students like Maurice about wrongdoing when they are afraid of the personal consequences of such a confrontation. When was the last time you hesitated to correct a student for fear that the student might retaliate? Many of you can identify with this or know a teacher who felt this way.

Many teachers also lack the skills needed to manage disruptive behavior in their classrooms. Counselors often hesitate to set limits for appropriate behavior, fearing that students will perceive them to be disciplinarians. As a result, boundaries for appropriate behavior become blurred. Students quickly develop a sense of which faculty and staff they can take advantage of, testing by pushing the limits of what is and what is not acceptable. Maurice may well have known that he could "face down" those two teachers in the hallway. You have also probably seen this in classrooms where teachers have lost control. Little academic work occurs, with teachers struggling to maintain order. Class rules, if they exist, may simply be posted on the board and ignored. No one has internalized or agreed to the rules. Subsequently, students either passively resist a teacher's attempt to engage them in some type of learning or openly refuse to participate. As things get more chaotic, the environment becomes more conducive to violent or aggressive behavior.

Counselors, teachers, and administrators have a reputation for going above and beyond the call of duty. Many spend countless hours helping students beyond what their contracts stipulate, either by offering extra help before or after school, or by sponsoring student clubs or after-school activities. Mr. Evans has supervised an after-school homework club for years. Mr. Evans has rethought this commitment, however, after being confronted with an angry student in a deserted hallway late one afternoon. Professionals who feel vulnerable are less likely to provide additional services, preferring instead to retreat from the "war zone" as quickly as possible at the end of the school day. Sound familiar? When was the last time you stayed late to work at school, with perhaps only a few people present in your building? And if your building is safe, how about your colleagues in other schools—ever hear any of them reflect about the safety in their schools after hours?

For some schools, preserving safety and maintaining control takes precedence over the school's mission to educate. Energy becomes directed at managing student behavior and guarding safety rather than education. Many schools have installed metal detectors at entrances and employ guards or even police for security. Many of you work in schools where this has become standard procedure. Although the school's staff may begin to perceive such actions as routine, these daily reminders can reinforce the feeling that school is a dangerous place. The financial support required by these extra security measures also directs resources away from educational programs.

Student Responses

Just like counselors, teachers, and staff, students may experience intimidation and fear at school. This may lead to avoidance of certain parts of the building—such as bathrooms, the locker rooms, or the cafeteria, where monitoring of student behavior is less extensive. As many of you know, it is not unheard of for some students to skip lunch or avoid the use of a bathroom for the entire school day out of fear. Skipping classes or staying home to minimize stress are also possibilities. Recently, the second author supervised a school counseling intern who was working with a high school student who was frequently absent. On the surface, health issues seemed to be the primary cause, and as the student missed more school, he fell farther and farther behind academically. These were concerns that needed to be addressed. However, as the counseling work continued, the student's fear of being bullied at school emerged as a major impediment to returning to school on a regular basis. Subsequently, the counselor's focus with this student shifted from academic failure, future goals, homework assignments, and so on, to the student's fear of violence.

One of the more subtle effects of violence on students is the attitude that students develop that violence is an acceptable way to solve problems. Such youngsters begin to think that using violence to solve problems is the normal way of doing things. This became very clear to the second author several years ago when working in an urban middle school. Most students who attended this school needed to use public transportation to get to and from school. Eighth-grade students reported that they were being harassed verbally by senior high students who boarded the same buses. Given that this school is located in a city with one of the highest juvenile murder rates in the country, the potential for violence was all too real.

Working with the eighth-grade students on conflict resolution skills and impulse control was one of the approaches the school decided to take to address the problem. Students learned a problem-solving process and were asked to develop role-plays demonstrating the use of these skills. Riding the bus was one of the focal areas for role-plays. Of course, as most of you know, students in middle school love to role-play, but not necessarily to demonstrate what you intend! In this particular case, the students concocted a role-play in which a high school student (Darryl) had a gun slightly visible in his coat pocket. Darryl approached the eighth grader (Larry) on the bus and requested that Larry move and give up his seat. It was surprising that even when Larry knew of the gun, he still refused to move. Now, of course, in the role-play, Larry very magically got the gun away from Darryl and managed to keep his seat. It was in probing with Larry about why he chose to resist and go for the gun that the issue of self-esteem and the need to be respected at all costs became very clear.

Frequently, adolescents see fighting and other acts of aggression as acceptable solutions to conflicts. Some students view the idea of self-protection and "do unto others before they do unto you" as an acceptable reason for the use of violence. As counselors, teachers, and administrators, many of you have probably had similar conversations with students who view violence as acceptable if used to protect one's dignity or sense of self-respect. Maintenance of respect is critical; handling threats to one's self-respect immediately and physically seems justified. Larry, the eighth-grade student ready to put his life on the line for his seat on the bus, illustrates this point. Some students fail to think of a violent act that is aimed at preserving respect, providing protection, or defending oneself against another's aggression as wrong. We suspect that your experiences with students support this.

Elijah Anderson, a well-known sociologist, has suggested that many inner-city youths are embedded in the street culture, where respect is difficult to achieve, can be lost easily, and must be guarded constantly. With the right amount of respect, a youth can avoid being bothered in public. Yet if he or she is bothered or "dissed" (disrespected), it becomes important to show that he or she is not someone to be "messed with." Physical force becomes an important vehicle for sending this message.

These examples underscore the volatile nature of the school environment. They also emphasize the importance of teaching students problem-solving and conflict resolution skills, but with the recognition that teaching these skills alone is insufficient. School counselors need to recognize that in addition to teaching students these skills, student attitudes about the acceptable use of violence must also be confronted. It will also be important for prevention programs to address the profound need that many youths have for self-respect, and to develop avenues for young people to acquire respect in legitimate, safe ways.

Summary

No one would argue that youngsters today are growing up in a more violent society. Schools can no longer think of themselves as immune from the problem of violence. The effects on faculty and students of working in a danger zone can impede a school's ability to focus on its educational mission. Chapter 2 explores the personal and contextual factors that place students at risk for developing aggressive behavior and examines the steps that schools are taking to preserve faculty and student safety.

Additional Reading Sources

American Psychological Association. (1993). *Violence & youth: Psychology's response, Volume 1: Summary report of the American Psychological Association Commission on Violence and Youth.* Washington, DC: Author.

Anderson, E. (1994, May). The code of the streets. *Atlantic Monthly,* pp. 81-94.

Centers for Disease Control and Prevention. (1995). *Health-risk behaviors among our nation's youth: United States, 1992* (DHHS Publication No. PHS 95-1520). Hyattsville, MD: U.S. Department of Health and Human Services, National Center for Health Statistics.

National Center for Education Statistics. (1998). *Violence and discipline problems in U.S. public schools: 1996-97* (NCES 98-030). Washington, DC: Government Printing Office.

2

Roots of Violence and Aggression

In looking at the issue of school violence, our picture would not be complete if our camera lens failed to capture what is happening in a student's life that places the student at risk of developing aggressive and violent behavior. Many of you know and work with students who get angry with little provocation and are quick to react, "get in someone's face," shout verbal abuses, or even hit another person as a means of rectifying a perceived wrong or asserting a need for power and respect. For some, the violent or aggressive act is an impulsive response to a perceived threat; for others, the act is a calculated means of revenge for an earlier wrong. Yet the behavior we see suggests little about how students develop such patterns of responding.

Violence is a very complex, multifaceted problem. Although many factors may contribute to why youngsters become violent, no one can say for sure what causes someone to be violent. The best we can do is to pinpoint factors that seem to be related to violent behavior and, when present in an individual's life, place that individual at greater risk for such behavior. Individual predisposition, personality tendencies, school environment, family relationships, and community and neighborhood characteristics all contribute to why certain individuals are more prone to violent behavior.

Individual Factors

From an individual perspective, certain types of temperament might, at an early age, place an individual on a path toward violent behavior. Other factors might include impulsivity, lack of empathy for others' feelings, a belief that factors beyond the individual's control are responsible for behavior, and a history of being a victim of violence. Given that impulsivity has a relationship to violence, youngsters who stop and think might be less likely to choose a violent alternative, whereas youngsters with attention-deficit hyperactivity disorder may be more vulnerable.

Peer Group Factors

An individual's peer group may also place him or her at risk. Janet was new to the school and eager to make friends. She was easily accepted into a group that she found to be exciting and much more daring than her friends from her former school. Although fighting wasn't something in which she ever got involved at her old school, she felt a certain respect for how her new friends weren't afraid to stand up for themselves, even if it meant a fight. Clearly, this was something new for Janet. The principles of modeling and social learning are at work when youngsters socialize with others who use violence and aggression to achieve desired outcomes. Janet's association with her new peers supports this principle. Soon, Janet adopted the aggressive postures and verbal remarks of her new friends. A member in her new group, who deliberately hurts someone, sets a norm for expected group behavior. Youngsters who join gangs are particularly vulnerable because the modus operandi for the majority of gangs includes violence. Although Janet would not describe her new group of friends as a gang, group members supported fighting as an acceptable way to resolve conflicts. Janet was eventually suspended for provoking a fight and hitting a classmate over what seemed to be a minor disagreement. It was later learned that the attack by Janet was prompted by her need to be included in the group and was a rite of passage. This is not uncommon, with peer groups requiring different behaviors, sometimes violent ones, in order to be initiated and accepted by peers. In fact, there may be serious repercussions for group members who fail to uphold the group code of behavior.

Family Factors

Parents who demonstrate poor self-control and aggressive and violent behavior become role models for their children. Carla's mother admits that she has a hard time getting Carla to do what she wants her to do, and that a quick swat seems to be the best motivator. It is no surprise that Carla's first response when a classmate refuses to do what she wants him or her to do is to reach over and pinch the other child on the arm. It has been suggested that this type of aggression develops over time as the child navigates a family system characterized by harsh, inconsistent discipline; poor supervision; inadequate parental modeling; and overall poor management of the child's aggressive and noncompliant behavior. Youngsters who grow up in these circumstances have little opportunity outside of school to learn positive ways to respond to conflict. Doing what comes naturally for such youngsters includes aggressive behavior that is learned as a routine part of their socializing experience. Some of you have probably worked with students like Michael, a fifth grader. Picking fights is how Michael solves problems. If he doesn't get his own way, his frustration generally leads to some type of physical or verbal confrontation. Shouting, use of foul language, and hitting are common reactions for Michael. Students like Michael often have a very limited array of responses when feeling angry, provoked, or dissatisfied in some way. Aggressive physical and verbal responses are customary. With older students, confrontational body language is also common.

Some students' aggression is rooted in response styles characterized by volatility, short fuses, and a tendency to overattribute hostile intent to others' intentions. Sam was a student who typified this aggressive pattern. Sam believed he was never wrong or at fault, saying things like, "Not my fault. . . . I didn't do it. . . . Yea, ask him what happened." Quick to anger, Sam was removed from more PE classes for fighting than any other student. When queried about the behavior that led to his dismissal, Sam took no responsibility for the problem. "Hey, they just keep saying things and bumping into me on purpose." The other students, from Sam's perspective, were always out to get him, setting him up for failure or ridicule. Some experts suggest that the aggressiveness of students like Sam, who fit this more reactive aggressive pattern, may be the result of having experienced abuse or the stress of living in high-crime neighborhoods.

Families may also contribute to a student's violent or aggressive behavior by accepting their child's use of such behavior as a problem-solving strategy. Many of you have probably encountered parents who encourage their child to hit back or to hit first if he or she is teased or bullied. Many times, we have heard parents or guardians say to us, "Don't want my kid to be pushed around. No way. I always tell him/her, if someone messes with you, I don't care who it is, push right back!" School counselors, teachers, and administrators who make efforts to teach and impart to students some coping strategies that are nonviolent may place themselves in direct opposition to a parent's directives.

School Factors

Schools have also come under scrutiny as contributing to violent behavior. Learning difficulties further complicate an already stressful life experience for the violence-prone student and unavoidably contribute to a student's feelings of powerlessness. The school's actual physical space may be conducive to aggressive behavior. How many of you work in buildings where student fights erupt during the normal changing of classes due to tight hallways and limited space for passing from one class to the next? It is no surprise that architectural firms are springing up that specialize in public school environments and are aimed at creating communities that emphasize learning and a healthy social climate.

School rules that require rigid and unquestioned conformity may also routinely lead to feelings of anger, resentment, and rejection. We would add that this would be particularly relevant to rules that are designed for heightening control without making sense to students. When this happens, students don't internalize or "own" the rules, and staff are simply enforcing the rules to maintain social control without an emphasis on the betterment of the school community. Often, in these instances, the rules become punitive whereby many staff assume moments of policing the environment to enforce the rules rather than educating students.

Community Factors

Certain community and neighborhood characteristics can also enhance a youngster's proclivity for violent behavior. Access to firearms is a factor in many youth homicides. The American Psychological Association estimates that nearly 50% of American households have firearms, and that half of these are handguns. It also estimates that about 270,000 students carry guns to school each day. The availability of these guns to a youngster who typically employs violent and aggressive behaviors in social situations causes a greater likelihood that angry or aggressive encounters may result in a lethal outcome. Being able to access firearms presents young people, many of whom may already feel powerless, with a way to feel more powerful, but a way that may lead to a deadly outcome. Regardless of why someone brings a gun to school—protection, revenge, or respect—possession of a lethal weapon in the hands of someone who is already at risk for violent behavior can be devastating.

Communities where alcohol is easily available to underage youngsters also places the youngsters who live in those communities at higher risk for violent encounters. Agreement exists among professionals that there is a connection between alcohol and other drugs and youth violence. Whether the use of these substances causes violent behavior, however, is less clear. Current thinking seems to suggest that use of alcohol makes a person less inhibited and thereby increases the likelihood for violence. Therefore, if you knew that Dominic, who was argumentative and aggressive with his peers in school, was regularly drinking on weekends, you would be aware that there may be a greater chance that he would become violent when drinking. This, in turn, would affect the way that you provide intervention strategies for him. This will be discussed more in Chapters 3 and 4.

Poverty is another factor that is linked with violent behavior. It is important to note that violence is linked with poverty regardless of race. What is it about poverty that leads to violence? Why do people living in poverty have a higher likelihood of using violence to solve problems?

Shelly is a good example. She spoke with her school counselor and shared how she doesn't have any hope. Her mother is unemployed, depressed, and drinks too much, always talking about how life could have been. Shelly can't control what is happening at home, and 2 years ago, at the age of 15, she gave up trying. Her older brother is involved "somehow" with drugs and is in and out of the house with his friends at all hours, and her younger brother is beginning to "run wild." She tried to study and keep up her grades until middle school, and then she gave up.

During her past few years in school, Shelly has grown to hate many of her peers, who come from more stable families and never seem to be stretched for money or clothes. Shelly is like many other poor students who lose hope, feel powerless, and are frustrated with the inequality that pervades her life. People like Shelly who see little opportunity for change in their life circumstances, who define themselves as the "have-nots" in a society of excess, and who feel that they lack the resources to achieve the outcomes they desire may become violent as an expression of their frustration and hopelessness. Shelly has been charged twice with physical assault and resisting arrest. She was caught stealing jewelry and makeup and became violent when undercover detectives tried to arrest her. Since then, she has joined a group of her peers that believes that violence is a way to take what they want and get things that are beyond their reach. Furthermore, Shelly perceives some people within the school and community as picking on her because she comes from an ethnic minority background and is poor; she shared with her counselor that she faces racism, discrimination, and inequality every day. This makes her "really angry," and she wants to lash out at those people.

There are other things that contribute to Shelly's discontent and rage. Neighborhoods with inadequate housing; high unemployment rates; high rates of crime and violence; and few or nonexistent community-based services, such as job training, day care, recreation, and public transportation, further contribute to her belief that violence is acceptable. Her mother, as with many other poor families, must often expend considerable energy just satisfying basic needs for food, shelter, and safety. We have found a number of younger children like Shelly's younger brother, Randy, living in high poverty areas who can't go outside their homes safely. Their families are scared that something might happen, and they, in turn, are afraid. Even more alarming is the large number of children like 10-year-old Randy, who was forbidden to stay in the front room of his apartment given the frequency of drive-by shootings in the neighborhood. When providing for basic safety and other fundamental needs, a family's energy may be exhausted. Providing further supervision and discipline to children may become secondary to caring for these more basic needs. Furthermore, youths like Shelly and her older brother, who live in such neighborhoods, may have greater limitations and opportunities for gainful employment, recreation, and facilities for extracurricular activities.

The prevalence of violence in the media is another factor that places youth at risk of violent behavior. Some of our most popular and successful movies, television programs, and music videos frequently use interpersonal violence as a major theme. Typically, they fail to portray the aftermath of the violence—the loss, grieving, mourning, and fear that often accompany a violent episode. Furthermore, violence is an integral part of some sporting events, with many athletic heroes earning reputations for being tough, no-nonsense people. Action figures, toy guns, and video games that depict heroes whose heroism is tied to the ability to destroy the enemy are a familiar part of many children's play world. Unfortunately, the message being communicated to the youth of today is clear—"Violence is everywhere, and it ain't so bad."

Violence Prevention

The complexity of factors that contribute to violent and aggressive behavior suggests that the problem is multidimensional with no single, simple solution. Knowing what places youngsters at risk is a first step in addressing the problem. Using this information to inform us about how we build and plan violence prevention programs is an important next step.

Faced with the challenge of preserving school safety, schools and school systems have responded in a number of ways, including the following:

1. Establishing policies and procedures that mandate strict punishments for infractions of school rules
2. Controlling access to school grounds and school buildings
3. Requiring visitors to sign in
4. Using metal detectors at school entrances
5. Conducting random metal detector checks
6. Using full-time or part-time security guards
7. Conducting drug sweeps

Used consistently, some of these measures may enhance school safety. How many of you, however, work in schools where ways to prevent weapons in the school are inadequate? You walk into the building or parking lot, unsure if some students might have weapons. In our visits to schools that have cameras, locked entrance doors, and policies for visitor sign-in, we have observed that policies are implemented inconsistently. Cameras, locks, and visitor sign-in procedures also fail to protect schools where the perpetrators are the students themselves. Schools also effect punishments such as suspensions and expulsions after a problem has already occurred. Punishments may be characterized as a deterrent, yet for those students who are prone to both violent behavior and impulsivity, the deterrent value may have little impact.

Schools have also initiated varied proactive prevention strategies, including teaching conflict resolution and problem-solving skills, and helping students to resolve conflicts peacefully through programs such as peer mediation and student court. Many of you are already familiar with these types of programs and are involved in their implementation. Many commercial curricula are available for developing these types of skills and for assisting school counselors in establishing peer mediation programs.

Given the variety of factors that place students at risk for violent behavior, we suggest that these strategies alone are insufficient to adequately address the problems. In addition to interventions that target students directly, it is important for prevention programs to also incorporate strategies aimed at change in the school, family, peer group, and community systems that support the learning and maintenance of violent and aggressive behavior. No single institution working alone has sufficient resources to effect such a comprehensive approach. We believe that this type of systemic change calls for an integrated, school-family-community prevention effort that incorporates strategies at the school, family, peer group, and community levels.

Building Offensive Strategies

Many of the steps that schools take to prevent violence and aggression are a reactive response to a problem that already exists. Although we are not suggesting that schools do away with measures to protect student and faculty safety, we do think that schools need to approach the problem proactively while also maintaining good interventions to more immediate problems. We believe that spending time and energy in developing good prevention programs is an investment in the future and time well spent.

We would concur with the suggestion that it is important to humanize the school environment by ensuring that teachers know about the communities where students live, understand issues of cultural diversity, and recognize and value individual student differences. Mr. Sharpe, the principal of a high school that has a history of violence, received a number of recommendations from his appointed committee to study violence in his school. Based on the report, he decided to take a new tack in dealing with this growing problem. He began by holding joint meetings with school faculty and staff and neighborhood community leaders to discuss common concerns, and initiating joint school-community events. In consultation with his staff, he found ways for family members to contribute time and talent to school activities in a meaningful way. This not only brought in families, some of whom were previously disengaged from the school, but also educated his own staff about the family strengths that might otherwise have gone unnoticed. Mr. Sharpe also actively demonstrated public and private appreciation for teachers and other staff who demonstrated keen sensitivities and an understanding about the unique factors in a student's life that contribute to violence. In fact, he called it a reeducation program for his staff that focused on not only an understanding of the problem, but also a subsequent change in value systems.

Both authors remember their first jobs working with impoverished youth. The first author worked in an Upward Bound antipoverty program where poverty, violence, suspensions from school, racism, and discrimination were rampant. He visited numerous homes and was involved in reeducating large numbers of staff from urban and rural schools. The second author has vivid memories of her first job as a school counselor in a rural community that included neighborhoods characterized by extreme poverty. Making a home visit was eye-opening. There was a great distance between the educator's academic expectations for completed homework each day and the five children who lived in a one-room dwelling without electricity and running water.

Creating new opportunities for parental involvement beyond the traditional parent-teacher conferences is another school-level change that is important to reduce violence. Ms. Jefferson was a good example of this. She was a single mother who had two children in the local elementary school. The school counselor got to know Ms. Jefferson through conversations and meetings between the two of them concerning the children's progress in school. During the school year, Ms. Jefferson lost her job and became increasingly depressed. The school counselor acted in a number of ways on Ms. Jefferson's behalf, including connecting her with an employment opportunity at the family resource center housed in the school building. Acquiring this new position not only solved an income problem for Ms. Jefferson but also relieved the stress she was under from the employment search process itself.

The same counselor recognized in Ms. Rice some tremendous yet untapped leadership qualities. When Ms. Rice was invited to participate on the school improvement team that addressed the problem of aggressiveness within the school, she was delighted. Including parents such as Ms. Rice in more nontraditional roles is another way that schools can invite parents to participate in reducing the problems of violence. Such a responsibility can be very empowering for a parent who might feel intimidated by the school and the authority it represents. Through such roles, a parent can become an integral and respected part of the school community.

Reaching beyond the school community is essential in reducing school violence. Planning and developing partnerships with community service providers (e.g., health, mental health, social services) to initiate school-based services and enhance communication and collaboration between school-based and community-based service providers is another powerful option. This strategy will be described in detail in Chapter 5.

Another important strategy focuses on paying particular attention to transition times, especially early adolescence and the move to middle school and high school environments. Although many of you already plan orientations for students entering middle and high school, we don't always think about this as an opportunity to reduce violence and aggression. Taking into account the stress for students and families during these times may help us reorient how we plan and offer these activities. For example, parent orientations that are more applicable for those more difficult-to-reach parents, children, and families at risk are important to develop. Orientation strategies may include (a) connecting parents with other parents, (b) providing a school directory with names and telephone numbers, (c) developing a parent advocacy program, (d) assigning family mentors, and (e) identifying telephone numbers of people in the school community to call about specific family problems.

Providing students with opportunities for learning not only nonviolent responses but also ways to develop positive relationships with peers and teachers is also important. Sandy Spring Middle School has all students take a 40-minute period per week of "Skills for Daily Living." Teachers and counselors provide instructions and facilitate group discussion on topics related to communication skills, developing empathy, problem solving, conflict resolution, and family life. Many schools have instituted character building as an integral part of the overall curriculum. School counselors not only teach some of the lessons but also team with teachers to provide support and encouragement for teachers who may be unsure about stepping into a new curriculum area. To facilitate a better sense of community, some schools have reorganized classes or grades to create smaller units or schools-within-schools. Each smaller unit may have its own administrative structure.

Helping Families

Providing accessible and affordable family counseling has been clearly linked to violence prevention and is imperative to reduce violent and aggressive behavior within and outside the home environment, including the school. Accessibility and affordability are essential concepts in providing services for families. Many schools are opting to locate community services within schools to provide easier access for parents. Some of you may work in schools that have formed school-community agency partnerships to provide such services. Linkages-to-Learning is a good example of one program that is based in a larger school system outside of Washington, DC. This program is a partnership between the school system, the Department of Health and Human Services, and local nonprofit agencies. The program provides school-based family counseling, case management, and home visits to minority and low-income families in identified neighborhoods. In some Linkages schools, the school counselor coleads counseling groups with the school-based agency clinician.

Some school counselors provide family counseling services to ameliorate family problems, including the reduction of aggressive behavior. If you are a practicing school counselor and want to move in this direction, you will need to be available during the hours when families have time, requiring that you restructure your workday.

For example, Ms. Bardsman, a school counselor in an urban school, has found that her work with families has significantly reduced school violence for a targeted population. She showed her principal the impact of her work with families and has now shifted her workday so that she works from 1:00 p.m. to 8:00 p.m., 3 days a week, instead of following more traditional school hours. The principal, rather than viewing her as not being available to fulfill her responsibilities, finds her work very important to the overall functioning of the school. Ms. Bardsman keeps the principal and the site-based management team apprised of the effects of her work, demonstrating the reduction in aggressive incidents for the students with whose families she is working; decreases in absenteeism, suspensions, and referrals to the principal; and of equal importance, improved grades. One thing that happened to Ms. Bardsman is that she realized a need for additional training in family counseling. You may also find the same to be true for you, because many school counseling programs do not require classes in this area; traditionally, training for school counselors focuses on theories and strategies designed to change individuals. Think about your own training program. We imagine that for most of you, much of what you studied addressed how to get individuals to change, with limited work on how to change the surrounding contexts that might contribute to an individual's problems. For at-risk students, both types of change are important and interrelated. School counselors who want to help students at risk for violence and aggression will want to incorporate a systems perspective into their counseling interactions. Chapter 5 elaborates on basic principles in systemic change.

Many school counselors provide parenting education, including skills for conflict resolution and maintaining discipline, all of which are related to issues of school violence. You may have had the experience of offering such training, only to be disappointed by having few parents attend. Taking such services directly into the community and collaborating with already established community service providers are ways that some counselors have increased participation. The school counselor at Blue Ridge Elementary School meets weekly to provide parenting education in the community room of a local public housing project. A social worker on the staff of the housing authority coleads the groups.

Parent mentoring programs that pair more experienced parents with parents who are less experienced, or more isolated in the community, are another effective option for reducing school violence. Beth, a former school counselor who now directs a regional family resource center, developed such a program by recruiting parents who lived in neighborhoods with high numbers of students at risk for school failure to be host parents. Host parents were employed by the school system and functioned as home-school liaisons. Connecting teachers and the school counselor with hard-to-reach parents, providing parenting support in the home, encouraging parent participation at school events, providing transportation to such events, and helping parents follow through on school recommendations are some of the host parents' responsibilities. Beth oversees and supervises the host parents, but the responsibility for the parent-to-parent contact within the community resides with the host parents. Establishing school-based family resource centers is another way to provide accessible support for families.

Peer Group Challenges

Although it might be tempting to propose transplanting an aggressive youth from a peer group that may be contributing to and supporting the youth's behavior to another, more positive group, a change in peer group isn't always a realistic alternative. Young people seek out and associate with peers who help meet their social and emotional needs, and the bonds are strong. A youth's peer group becomes a vehicle for passage from childhood to adulthood. Identifying with a peer group provides a sense of security at a time of normal development, when the young person is moving away from an identity with parents. This movement can be a healthy process. It can become unhealthy, however, when a young person identifies with a peer group that supports dangerous behavior. Trying to disengage a youth from his or her peer group will be met with extreme resistance. In most instances, successful interventions need to target the peer group itself by helping the group as a whole find positive ways to meet members' needs for belonging and self-worth. Chapter 4 provides strategies for peer group intervention through structured group work.

It is also important for schools to provide opportunities for students to satisfy their need for belonging and self-worth through activities that connect them with other peers and caring adults. Creating more opportunities for students to achieve success in school both academically and nonacademically can enhance a student's feeling of being connected to the school community. Receiving recognition for accomplishments from school staff, peers, and family members empowers students in a positive way. A group of students at Carlton High School wanted to do something to help diminish the violence and aggression that was on the increase among students at their school. With the help of a faculty sponsor, the students developed an improvisation company that now holds performances at Carlton and other local schools. The main theme of their drama skits was how to resolve conflicts peacefully.

The process of connecting young people becomes as important as the activity through which the connection is made. When one well-known educator investigated what made prevention programs successful, she discovered from interviews with recipients of program services that the relationship with the agency or school and people in the agency or school who are providing the services was as important as the service itself! If we understand this information and incorporate it into the programs we are developing, we would certainly include programs that emphasized the need for children and adolescents to belong and feel positive about themselves through their relationships with the adults administering programs as well as their peers. We pose to you, the reader, the challenge of examining the opportunities that exist at your school to facilitate these connections, especially because this has been found to be essential for the student who is most vulnerable to violence and aggression. Another associated issue that we have found in our work with schools is the struggle with limited financial resources that inhibit adequate transportation so that students can participate in after-school activities. This was a problem at Jones Landing High School, and many students who could have benefited from more involvement in extracurricular activities were unable to participate. To tackle this, the school principal invited the county public transportation system to engage in joint problem solving about this issue, and they came up with some solutions that addressed this concern.

Creating Safe Communities

An area where schools and communities can cooperate in violence prevention is the support of joint recreational activities at neighborhood facilities. This permits youth to spend time in a structured environment with healthy activities and adult supervision. Horace, a ninth grader, regularly participates in activities offered at community recreation centers and youth sports teams. Although he is not a strong academic student, this offers him opportunities in leadership training and development. At the same recreation center is Henry, an 11th grader who attends the same school as Horace. Henry serves as peer mentor to Horace. He is mentoring Horace at the recreation center and in middle school as one of the requirements for his service learning hours. The school counselor provides leadership, coordination, and training for the mentoring program in which both Horace and Henry are involved.

Gun control is a very volatile political issue, yet implementing gun and other weapon control measures is closely tied to the prevention of violent crimes. There are many ways that communities can become involved in addressing this problem. One way has been to develop media campaigns (brochures, radio and TV announcements, talk shows, newspaper announcements) that provide information to the public about positive alternatives to conflict and tips for gun safety. These messages must be geared toward youth and families and provide a succinct and clear communication. School counselors, teachers, and administrators can be of great assistance in developing these messages. Also, school personnel can advocate for changes in public policy related to the use of, and access to, weapons.

Finally, schools and communities can join together to provide employment and volunteer opportunities that allow youths to contribute in a tangible way to their community. Jed got a summer job at a local garden center through a cooperative vocational training program between his high school and several businesses in the community. Some of his friends received placements with plumbers, carpenters, hair stylists, and librarians.

At this point, you are probably asking yourself how school counselors, teachers, or school administrators can do all of these things. They can't! Joint efforts among schools, families, and communities are critical. Chapter 5 elaborates on how schools and school counselors can provide leadership for establishing such partnerships.

Needed: Multiple Skills

In addition to implementing strategies that affect multiple contexts with regard to violence prevention, it is also important for prevention programs to teach more than problem-solving skills. Students prone to violent and aggressive behavior generally experience a broad range of maladaptive behaviors. Consequently, prevention programs need to provide training for multiple skills, including problem solving, conflict resolution, verbal and nonverbal communication, assertiveness, anger management, and more general social skills. What we have learned studying these areas is that one-shot or short-term programs are not effective; rather, the programs will be effective if they are delivered over a longer period of time where there is continual practice and reinforcement of the new skills. This means that we should keep in mind that length of time and number of times we try out what we are learning leads to greater success and program effectiveness. If you are currently offering such programs or plan to do so, it would be good to rethink your time commitment to ensure that you have allotted a sufficient amount of time to achieve the desired effects.

Rob, the school counselor at Greendale Elementary School, was asked to work with a particularly difficult group of third-grade students. The number of discipline referrals for fighting was quite high for this group, and Rob, the teachers, and the school principal felt that some early intervention would be helpful. Rob developed a schedule that included short-term, skills-based group counseling for four, 8-week increments, with each 8-week session followed for several weeks by less formal meetings. Skills were introduced and practiced in the group sessions and then reinforced during the less structured time through observations in the classroom and at recess time. Family members were contacted at the beginning and end of each 8-week session so that Rob could share plans, note student improvement, and encourage family support. Rob also consulted with the local recreation center director to strategize how skills might be reinforced in general with all of the students who frequent the center. Rob plans to continue his work with this group next year when they move to the fourth grade.

Although there are some generalizations that we can make about the causes of aggressive behavior, the specific reasons why each aggressive student behaves this way is individualized. This means that we must, to some degree, tailor the type of skill training that would be most effective for each student. It is important for youngsters who are aggressive and who view that as a normal response pattern to feelings of frustration, anger, sadness, resentment, jealousy, and so on to learn alternative problem-solving strategies. Rob provided this type of training in his group by helping students learn a structured problem-solving process that included identifying the problem, stopping to think, thinking of alternatives, and evaluating possible consequences. Many of you already provide this type of training. We encourage you, though, to remember that we know that the most effective training needs to occur for a long period of time with repeated doses. Remember that Rob planned to deliver his intervention over the course of a year in incremental stages. Some of you may feel that this is a real luxury to be able to work this intensely with a single group of students. We believe that it is an important investment over time for long-term change, and we remind you that there are no quick fixes. What was important for Rob was that he had secured both his principal's and teachers' commitments to this work as a priority for these students and Rob's program for the academic year. Helping the families of youngsters who exhibit aggression assists in creating discipline structures within the family that empha-size negative consequences for aggressive behavior and reinforce nonaggressive behavior. This can be seen in Rob's periodic meetings with Marvin's mother. Marvin was one of Rob's group members who had a particularly difficult time containing his aggressive outbursts. Rob discovered that Marvin's mother was also having trouble with Marvin's anger at home. Together, they developed an agreement between Marvin and his mother. Marvin could earn TV time and praise for "keeping his cool" when responding to his mother's re-quests, particularly when he is upset. TV time was lost when Marvin failed to contain his outbursts. It was extremely important for Rob to follow up with Marvin's mother on a regular basis. Just like Marvin, she, too, was learning new behavior that Rob needed to reinforce through positive comments and attention. School counselors who provide such help should remember that reinforcing the teacher or parent who is helping the child to manage his or her aggression is just as important as direct work with the child. Shaping adult behav-ior is critical for an eventual change in the student's behavior and relates to both the home and the school.

For those students who fit a more reactive aggressive pattern, developing skills for anger management, social role taking, and empathy are important. The second author worked in a group con-text with a very bright first-grade boy, Joey, who fit this type of aggressive pattern. Joey was one of four first graders who partici-pated in this group. All had difficulty with appropriate social skills and exhibited differing degrees of aggressiveness. The group used play activities that would elicit typical problem behaviors from the students. At first, when playing a board game, Joey never even considered that someone else might like to have the first turn, or that there would be any reason why he shouldn't move all of the pieces for each of the players. On more than one occasion, if he didn't get his way, he would slam his fist into the board, scattering the pieces. Winning was all-important, and accusing others of cheating was common. To think about how someone else might feel as a result of his behavior was not within his grasp at first. Through a process that encouraged an interplay between activity and discussion, re-inforcement of appropriate behavior, and an introduction of concrete skills, Joey slowly began to replace impulsive actions with stopping to think, and aggressive actions with congenial words.

As you review your school's violence prevention program, you might want to assess whether or not it includes some of the different dimensions suggested in this chapter. It takes a considerable amount of time and skill to implement the type of broad-based program suggested here. School counselors, teachers, and administrators may have the skills but, unfortunately, do not always have the time to engage in ongoing counseling or teaching relationships with students who have such complex needs as those for whom violence and aggression are a chronic problem. Counselors supposedly have a more focused training regarding students with deep-seated emotional difficulties; teachers are considered more knowledgeable about classroom management; and principals, by virtue of their experience as educators and sometimes their role, are thought to be competent to handle violence. Yet this is not always true. Not only may the training and skills be missing, but any of these professionals may lack the time and training to plan, implement, and coordinate the type of extensive violence prevention programs suggested here. Undertaking this work often involves learning new skills while simultaneously learning about the basis for violent and aggressive behavior and developing strategies for prevention and intervention. Even so, it is a crucial undertaking.

Summary

Changing the service delivery structure and priorities for your school counseling program may be an essential first step in being able to effect some of the changes suggested here. This may require negotiating with your administrator as well as positioning yourself politically within the school through participation on the school's decision-making committees or teams. Sally, the school counselor at River's Edge, exemplifies this point. The school-family-community mental health team at River's Edge identified establishing a school-based family resource center as a prevention priority. Sally coordinated the planning for the center with team members from the Department of Social Services. Launching such a center takes a considerable amount of time—time that the school's principal, recognizing the long-range benefits of such a center, allotted to Sally. Once operational, institutionalizing the center within the structure of the school became important. To accomplish this, Sally worked to incorporate the center into the school improvement team's plan for the following year. Sally is a member of this site-based management team.

Unfortunately, violent and aggressive behaviors are a reality that schools must face. Recent data seem to indicate that crime and violence do appear to be escalating in schools across the country. However, schools, through their school counselors, teachers, and administrators, are not powerless. Many schools have instituted measures to protect students and staff, and many have initiated violence prevention programs. It is important to remember that programs to deter such a complex problem need to be multidimensional, long term, and far reaching.

We have now had a chance to examine factors that appear to influence violent and aggressive behavior, and the implications this has for school prevention programs. In the next chapter, we will bridge the gap between what counselors are trained to do and what counselors need to be able to do to work effectively with students who are either potentially aggressive or violent or at the edge of such an episode.

Additional Reading Sources

Dodge, K. (1991). The structure and function of reactive and proactive aggression. In D. Pepler & K. Rubins (Eds.), *Development and treatment of childhood aggression* (pp. 210-218). Hillsdale, NJ: Lawrence Erlbaum.

Larson, J. (1994). Violence prevention in the schools: A review of selected programs and procedures. *School Psychology Review, 23,* 151-164.

Schorr, L. (1997). *Common purpose: Strengthening families and neighborhoods to rebuild America.* New York: Doubleday.

3

Learning to Help: On-the-Job Training

Those of us who are school counselors attended graduate school and took courses that helped us become professionals. We learned many skills in school about individual and group counseling, career counseling, testing and assessment, guidance programs, human development, personality theory, and working with families, to mention just some of our training background.

Even with this comprehensive curriculum, there are still large gaps between what we learned and the real world of the school. The topic of this book—aggressive and violent youth—is one area that most counselor education programs do not include in their training. In fact, the multitude of case examples that we studied during our training, as well as our clients and issues during practica and internship, frequently do not even mention this very important issue. What results is that most school counselors, teachers, and administrators lack any exposure to these concerns and the subsequent understanding and skills to effectively work with violent and aggressive students. Yet violence and aggression have been identified as critical problems in schools throughout the United States. The irony is that the most often called-upon professional to deal with crises in schools is the school counselor. Untrained and frequently lacking the tools to intervene adequately, but having the closest skills to manage and diffuse a violent or dangerous student, counselors often find themselves asked to handle these volatile, potentially violent, or already violent situations with aggressive students.

The result of not having the training and experience with issues of violence and aggression has caused a forced and rapid need to learn on the job. We know from national statistics and reported incidents of violence, as mentioned in Chapters 1 and 2, that you will certainly be faced with aggressive students and, sometimes, aggressive and angry family members. This holds true in urban, suburban, and rural areas, for both upper-income and low-income districts, and in areas with predominantly white students as well as areas with high concentrations of minority students. The situation is universal. The critical question, then, is what happens when you are faced with these situations and you are the only person—with all of your good communication skills, intuition, confrontation, empathy, and listening skills, but little or no training or track record—in this realm of anger and aggression. The hope, of course, is that somehow, all of your training and personal skills will carry you through these precarious situations so that you can reach the angry or scared students or family members, but there are limits to success without better preparation or guidance. This chapter discusses how you might better apply the counseling skills you already have and learn more quickly while on the job.

Self-Scanning: What Are You Thinking?

The first question to always ask yourself when working with a violent or aggressive student is, "What am I thinking?" This comes before doing anything, reacting in any way, or saying anything. This type of quick self-reflection becomes automatic for counselors, and it provides a quick, momentary self-scan. What am I thinking and feeling at this moment? The self-scan takes only seconds but provides important data for the upcoming intervention. You can learn from the scan about what is going on within you, and you can get a quick read on your reaction to the angry student. The insight you gain from this deeper level review will not only help you to understand yourself, but it will also give you information that helps you to feel what the student is experiencing at that moment. This information, based on your reaction, is essential in helping you to understand in a deeper, unconscious way what might be going on for the student. For example, if you feel like bolting from the room as you approach a student, it might be a signal that the student is really on the brink of violence, rather than just being loud to get attention. On the other hand, if you feel like you had better tread softly as you enter the room, it may be that the student is really not as prone to violence as he or she appears. What is important here is to trust your self-questioning and use the answers and awareness to help formulate what intervention would be most appropriate at that moment with that student.

The ability to self-scan in moments when there are high energy and strong feelings is a skill that will develop over time. You will probably find that self-scanning at first takes a concerted effort, similar to really listening for the beginning counselor. When you begin to work with violent students, your first inclination might be to allow the fear, anger, frustration, or feelings of helplessness to engulf you. To slow down and spend the quick seconds scanning will be an effort, but an effort that will help you to better find a window into the world of the violent student. As you practice, you will become better at doing this. You will find that trusting what you are thinking becomes a crucial link to a better understanding and connection with the student.

Goals: Where Are You Going?

You will probably find it helpful to consider what your goals and priorities are with the angry student during the situation. This is something that, once again, one does not learn in counselor education programs or in-service training. Rather, it develops as an important skill once you are on the job. This is especially true because school personnel such as school counselors, administrators, and certain teachers are identified as being able to handle crisis situations. For example, take the crisis situation that is presented to counselors, teachers, and administrators hundreds, if not thousands, of times a day in the United States. You are walking down the hallway headed for the lunchroom and see a violent, angry student walking by. You, the staff member, must give up your break time and decide what to do instantaneously. Other students are at risk of getting hurt, property could be damaged, the upset student could be hurt, and you may be injured in an altercation. To add to that, you might even realize that this situation, if it escalates, may get local, regional, or even national attention. It is up to you to manage, because you are the person there at that moment. No other faculty or staff member is around. It is important to decide quickly not only what you will do, but also what you want to accomplish. Naturally, the goal is to diffuse the situation and calm the student. However, the goals in a violent situation must be broken down even more so that you define to yourself the next immediate small step that will lead to the overarching goal. The self-scanning must take place first and is best followed by a split-second decision with small step goals. The goals you will be aiming for should take only seconds to define to yourself.

Typically, there is a sequence of four goals that you should consider. They are defined as follows:

1. *Goal 1: The safety of those students and staff who are nearby.* They must not be hurt as a result of the presenting situation, and it may be your first priority to "clear the decks." An example of this is the time the first author found himself facing a student who was threatening to throw a desk. The student was yelling, loud, and angry. Quickly, a crowd gathered around him, some simply observing what was going on, others taunting him, and others insisting that he "get it together." The situation was chaotic, with the possibility that the confusion around the student would escalate into a violent and harmful scenario. The job at hand was to ensure environmental safety so that the

observers would neither get hurt nor further exacerbate the situation.

2. *Goal 2: Ensuring that you, the school counselor, are not in a dangerous position where you could be physically trapped and possibly hurt.* There have been many times when a school counselor or other staff member was inadvertently cornered in a room or corridor and was unable to get away from a violent student. It is very important to place yourself in a position that is not threatening to the student; you do not want to be trapped in a place where you cannot back away or actually get out if necessary. The ability to move away from an aggressive student may actually be the more effective goal in decreasing the violence, rather than a direct confrontation. Therefore, it is essential that the school counselor place himself or herself in a position where he or she can move and not be injured.

3. *Goal 3: Direct intervention with the aggressive student.* The aim here is to diffuse the situation and minimize the risk of harm to the student or anyone else. This goal happens after safely taking care of other people and ensuring that you are in the safest position possible to intervene with the student. Once Goals 1 and 2 have been reached, you must quickly decide what your intentions are with the aggressive student. Do you want the student to put down the weapon, leave the room with you, take a deep breath, express his or her outrage or sadness, take a walk together, ventilate? Even though this is a split-second decision, it should be done thoughtfully and with deep insight and understanding of the problem to the best of your ability with limited information.

To review your personal goals in helping aggressive students is essential. It must be underscored that this review and decision takes only seconds but provides a foundation for what you do in a critical moment. Only after you determine where you want to go can you effectively begin to move ahead.

4. *Goal 4: Protect property whenever possible.* This must be done carefully but with assurance and directness. For example, when

there are breakable objects stacked on a counter and the violent student is threatening to destroy things, it may be important to firmly ask the student to walk with you to another part of the room to talk. The first author has done this many times, and much to his surprise, the aggressive student has most often followed to another place that was determined to be safer.

An example of self-scanning and goal setting can be seen with a situation facing the first author. A troubled 17-year-old student was brought to his office one day. The student had a history of violence and was on the verge of exploding and threatening everyone around him, including the counselor. As they spoke, the student reached in his pocket and took out a small nail file that he was carrying. Although, at first glance, the file appeared rather benign, the potential for harm was all too real as the student waved it in the air, clutching it tightly and then slamming his fist into a desk. He was visibly upset, and it was obvious that he could transform the file into a weapon that he could use on someone or something if necessary. As the first author did his self-scanning, he realized that the student was truly dangerous at this moment, on the verge of losing control, and capable of using the file as a weapon on him should he be provoked. Being in touch with his own deeper reaction to the situation, the first author quickly reviewed and decided on his goals. It was important that his aims be accurately decided before he did or said anything. Not concerning himself at this moment with the weapon, he decided to help the student feel less trapped and enraged by trying to change the environment. He suggested they take a walk away from the building, the other students, and staff. This provided safety for others, removed the student from things that he might potentially destroy in his anger, and placed the counselor in a situation whereby he was not trapped in a closed space with the angry student. It also brought the student outside the building and moving, which had the potential, if handled correctly, to symbolically move him away from his anger. The first author continued to scan and watch the student's reactions as they walked and as the student began to relax with the file. They spoke softly together as they walked. Finally, with a huge sigh of relief, the student repocketed the nail file. The goal to remove him from the environment and quietly talk about his fury was important in handling the situation. If, on the other hand, the immediate goal had been to focus on the potential weapon and disarm the student, the situation would have quickly escalated with the probability of someone being hurt.

Alliance Building: Trust as a Key

One might ask, "Why did the first author go outside with the student in the preceding scenario?" The answer is very simple, yet it is one of the most difficult things we do when working with violent or aggressive youth. The attempt was to establish an alliance, a bond, so that we can start to break through the strong feelings and reactions of the student and so that he can begin to calm down. The difficulty in doing this is that we have not been trained how to establish an alliance with an aggressive, violent student. In our training, we learn about interpersonal relationships, helping skills, communication skills, and behavioral strategies to manage acting out in classes and school environments, and, sometimes, conflict resolution. We learn all of these skills through working with students who are generally more responsive to us. What we don't learn about and where we fall short is how to react when we face more extreme problems, such as angry and violent behavior. Once again, this brings us back to learning on the job.

One of the most important first steps that was illustrated in the example described above is to initiate an intervention intended to break through the student's strong feelings of anger and create an alliance. This alliance is most effective when created through a personal bond, an avenue that links you, the school counselor, teacher, or administrator, with the student on a more meaningful level. This is contrary to some contemporary thought, whereby the first line of response to violence or aggression in a school is to use force. Force has taken the shape of police in the schools, guards on site, or actual hired groups or gangs to provide a show of force within the school.

We suggest that the use of force might generate greater distancing and difficulties with the school between students and staff. Instead, we advocate that professionals must learn how to forge a purposeful connection with the violent student. This requires breaking through the emotional clutter that is predominant for the violent student at that time.

To penetrate the emotional turmoil of the violent student, skills are required. One cannot simply say, "Why don't you stop all this anger. Just calm down and let's talk." This will not work with the truly angry student. Rather, one must find a window through the student's emotional chaos. Reaching him or her means that we are addressing the deeper problem, rather than just doing patchwork and postponing the violence for another day.

Even when we realize that we must aim for an alliance rather than a forceful imposition of power that may trigger greater danger and harm, questions remain. "How do I reach a violent student to estab- lish trust?" "How am I able to break through all that behavior, defensiveness, anger, and sadness to find the person underneath and establish an alliance?" "What do I do?" These are important queries. To be able to establish trust, we need to be able to answer these questions. Although we have made some suggestions for how to go about this, complete answers can only come on the job.

When on the job, we must rely on our own instincts and observa- tions of colleagues to understand how to do this. We have learned in school about rapport and communication with students and col- leagues. Confrontation with a violent student is not anywhere in the textbooks and usually is not in the repertoire of our teachers and trainers. Yet we must acquire this skill quickly because we are regu- larly faced with students who are potentially aggressive if not overtly violent. Therefore, what must we do differently to reach the intense feelings of violent students to establish trust? We suggest three basic guiding principles:

1. *Watch thyself.* When a student is angry and volatile, we react. Our palms get sweaty, our jaws may tighten, we feel a knot in our stomachs, and our tone of voice may change. It is far more difficult to establish a sense of trust with the out-of-control

student when we are taut and emotionally and physically con-
stricted. When faced with a violent student, one of your first
reactions should be to watch yourself. If you learn to control
your physiological and emotional reactions, you stand a far
better chance of coming across to the student and creating more
trust. This is a skill that takes time and must be practiced.

2. *Grounded speaking.* Once you have taken stock of your body and
   your feelings, use your voice and words as an outward gesture
   toward the angry student. Everything that you say at this point
   must be grounded. You do not want to raise your voice and try
   to verbally overpower the student, who is most likely already
   feeling powerless. To accomplish your goal of creating an alliance with the student, who is isolated at this moment, you want
   a steady and direct tone, choosing words that will break
   through the emotional turmoil to establish a bond. This way of
   communicating is very important in fostering trust, and we call
   it "grounded speaking." The first author recalls seeing a sea-
   soned school staff member who was sitting in a chair being
   confronted with a violent student waving a knife in his face.
   The principal spoke with the aggressive student in a slow, direct
   manner. He was fully grounded as he spoke. Again, if he had
   lost that grounding, it is highly likely that he and other staff and
   students would have been severely hurt.

3. *Move slowly.* The third guiding principle is about movement. We
   are now watching ourselves and using grounded speaking, and
   the final element that will assist in bonding is movement. We
   must change our pace of movement so that the student will
   slow down enough to think about aligning with us. The student
   is on a fast pace, in emotional turmoil, and needs the environment around him or her to slow down. We become the focal
   point in the surrounding environment as we are able to penetrate the strong feelings of the student, and therefore, we must
   not only speak distinctly but also move slowly. The principal
   who was faced with the student with the knife sat in his chair
   without movement. He remained outwardly calm, checking his
   intense fear and bodily reactions so that he remained in an

unwavering posture. To remain sitting also placed the principal in a lower position physically, which could be perceived by the student as less threatening. Should he have moved, there is no doubt that he and others may have been stabbed and seriously injured.

Summary

    This chapter suggested that most counselors receive little training or support for intervening with volatile or potentially volatile students. Learning how to work with violent and aggressive students for the most part occurs on the job. We've introduced a self-scanning technique, four specific goals for maintaining safety, and strategies for forming alliances as essential elements in learning to help those who are experiencing a violent episode. Chapter 4 expands upon this theme by introducing principles for effective interactions with violent and aggressive students. Chapter 4 also explores how school counselors might use the dynamic of group process to explore the deeper issues connected with the violent student's behavior.

4

Innovative Interventions and Group Work

Typical Responses

There is a crisis in the school. Word gets to you that something is going on outside the school library. You hear that someone is about to explode, and there is a possibility that other students could get hurt. "Is it true?" You breathe faster, your mind becomes pinpointed on your concern, and you wonder if you can help in the situation. "Maybe someone is injured or about to be hurt." A quick memory about last year when someone did get hurt flashes through your mind. "Could this be a replay of that situation? That was awful! If only that time, if only that morning before the incident, I had . . . " Your mind is racing, and you wonder what could happen, what are the outside extremes. This barrage of thoughts takes only seconds, just coming at you. Just as quickly and almost simultaneously, you make a decision to move. You dart up from your chair and head toward the place where the problem is brewing.

Frequently, as counselors, we are heading into the thick of a potentially dangerous situation with a student who is either out of control or nearing this state. We may have great determination and a strong desire to deescalate this situation. Maybe we even have a large physique that would intimidate students because we may appear to be able to physically overpower and control them if necessary. We might have an authoritative voice that commands respect. Regardless, most of us do not carry the skills to manage a more complicated and dangerous situation. This is particularly confusing because our psychological and/or physical prowess may often assist us in resolving many situations. The problem occurs when the situation or student comes along who is further along the continuum, who is more violent and agitated. This situation requires not only our innate and learned-on-the-job abilities, but also another set of more sophisticated skills. It is in these instances that we find that our typical interventions prove to be ineffective; our usual repertoire of interventions is insufficient for the more serious violent incident.

Intervention Principles

There are six intervention principles that are helpful to keep in mind when intervening with aggressive students. These principles are an important foundation for communication and interaction and are essential in diminishing violent situations.

Intervention Principle 1: Success

This concept may sound simplistic and straightforward, but success is typically ignored as a premise for gauging interventions with aggressive students. Success occurs when the goals for which one is striving have, in fact, been accomplished. Frequently, we do not acknowledge the progress made in violent situations. Instead, we continue to insist that we gain full control over the situation rather than allow a process to unfold and the violence to deescalate as a result of that process. For example, Janine has been threatening loudly to beat up another student. She has been yelling in the hallway, has thrown a book against the locker, and is daring the other student to do something. You may be challenging her behavior and trying to calm her down. Janine angrily says, "OK, I won't throw anything, but she [the other student] is still gonna have to do it different." Where many counselors, teachers, and administrators get thrown here is that they don't keep pace with Janine to see that their intervention has some success at this point. She has agreed not to throw the book but is still threatening the other student. The key here is to keep pace and acknowledge her change. This means that instead of staying at the same pitch and intensity of the intervention so far, one must make shifts that are aligned with the major step that Janine just took. Rather than loudly demanding that Janine lower her voice and stop threatening the other student, the counselor, teacher, or administrator could slightly lower his or her voice and comment, "Great, you won't throw anything, Janine. What does she have to do different?" The lowering of your own voice and acknowledgment that Janine has made a significant step is crucial in communicating that you can see her success in gaining more control. To demand that she fully lowers her voice, change her tone, stop threatening, and so on is ignoring her success and may reescalate the situation.

Intervention Principle 2: Realistic Goals

When we are working with aggressive or violent students, we want everything to be controlled. This need for safety is often the driving force behind our behavior in these situations. When we are too focused on control, however, we run the risk of losing sight of other important issues. Thus, one important guiding principle is to not lose sight of what we are aiming to accomplish in a violent situation but to do this through smaller, realistic goals. A realistic goal does not mean total and full cessation of anger or aggression, but what it does acknowledge is that the situation is on its way to being diffused and under control. If we reconsider Janine's situation, our first goal might be that she stops throwing objects that may hurt someone. This is a first success. What we shouldn't expect is that Janine will immediately lower her voice, stop threatening her peer simply because we have arrived, and suddenly become contrite and respectful rather than angry and aggressive. If we focus at first on realistic, practical goals instead of the big picture, our chance of achieving small successes as identified in Principle #1 is greatly enhanced. If we do aim for more realistic goals as our objective, our chances of eventually meeting the overarching goal to prevent and/or stop violence is more likely to be achieved.

Intervention Principle 3: Short-Term Interventions

Coinciding with success and realistic goals are short-term interventions. The emphasis in any violent situation is to focus on short-term solutions. This is in line with the aim for quick successes that are small and achievable and lead toward the larger goal of completely diffusing the situation. Once again, Janine is a good example. We may know from personal discussions with Janine that she dislikes her mother's new boyfriend, who seems to take up too much of her mother's time. Janine feels neglected by her mother. We also may know that her mother has started to go out at night with her boyfriend, and that Janine was worried that this past weekend, her mother would be out very late or maybe not even come home. Even though we know all of this information about Janine, it would be inappropriate to start discussions about this as we find her in the hallway on a Monday morning, threatening another student. Rather, it is important to target short-term interventions by having her stop throwing anything or verbally provoking a fight where someone may be hurt. It would be unrealistic to expect her to sit quietly at that moment in the empty lunchroom and explore what happened during the weekend that may relate to her fury. Instead, we attempt to make a short-term intervention that will put boundaries on the violence and maintain a safe environment.

Intervention Principle 4: Teaming

Violent and aggressive students present difficulties in our work in schools. They have many other issues that interfere with the academic goals of schools and are not remedied easily. They come from a myriad of difficult situations with different problems that have prompted them to manage their worlds through violence, meaning that there isn't a simple solution or easy answer. For those with more acute problems, the traditional response of behavioral management is limited and frequently misses the depth of emotional turmoil that students face as they encounter their worlds. The confounding issues in their lives lead to our recommendation for a team approach to address their problems. We suggest that this be on two levels—one within the school and one with human resources from outside the school. Within the school, we are including the counselors, teachers, school psychologists, social workers, administrators, nurses, secretaries, custodians, cafeteria workers, safety personnel, and so on. Full teams have been shown to be far more effective in addressing the needs of aggressive children when compared to professionals working alone without larger team support. The composite intermingling of issues that these youths carry, in our opinion, require a multitude of professionals from differing areas of specialization to pool their expertise to address violence. The in-house school teams, with their diverse training, can better contribute to understanding and intervening successfully with an aggressive student. When the in-house teams find that they are not succeeding at prevention and intervention plans, then it is time to cooperate with professionals in the community. Individuals from mental health facilities, family treatment centers, substance abuse facilities, social services, child protective services, juvenile services, child advocacy groups, community police programs, and homeless shelters may provide valuable insight regarding what is going on with an aggressive child, as well as collaborative strategies for intervention (see Chapter 5).

An example of using teaming effectively may be seen in the case of Sam, an intelligent 15-year-old male who has been increasingly aggressive toward his peers, with rumors in school that he was physically threatening and occasionally assaulting some of them. He was arrested recently for stealing clothes from a department store. Trying to avoid arrest and get away from the security guard who blocked his exit from the store, Sam attacked him, resulting in a court-ordered, short-term juvenile services placement. Upon returning to school, a behavioral intervention plan designed by the school psychologist failed after 2 weeks. Sam commented that "that plan was stupid." The school counselor, feeling at a dead end, called together a team of Sam's teachers, the principal, the school psychologist, and the school-family outreach worker. In this meeting, the members learned that Sam's mother had lost her job just before the stealing incident. Since that event, Sam's mother was sitting at home, depressed and inactive. It was further reported by the family outreach worker that Sam had begun counseling at the local mental clinic. This information prompted the school counselor to call a larger meeting with the caseworker from juvenile services and the mental health counselor (after the family outreach worker received a written release from Sam's mother). The meeting provided an avenue for all professionals involved with Sam to communicate their concerns and to work together toward a comprehensive intervention plan. At the meeting, the juvenile services caseworker and the mental health counselor shared with the school personnel that Sam was taking care of his mother emotionally, and he had stolen the clothes to spare both of them the embarrassment of not being able to afford them. The school counselor and outreach worker shared Sam's lack of progress in school and his increasing tendency toward violent interactions with his peers. As a result of this meeting, several steps were taken to help Sam and his mother. Both the mental health counselor and the school counselor agreed to work with Sam on recognizing his anger before it escalated to a violent or aggressive reaction; both also agreed to help Sam recognize positive actions that he might take when he feels that he is losing control. The mental health counselor also agreed to spend time addressing some of the underlying problems that contribute to Sam's feelings of hostility. The juvenile services worker assumed responsibility for monitoring Sam on a weekly basis to ensure that he kept his appointments with the mental health counselor and arranged for Sam's transportation to and from these appointments. The school-family outreach worker agreed to maintain contact with Sam's mother and encouraged her to seek support services for herself, while the outreach worker connected Sam's mother with the local community job search program. All agreed to reconvene in 3 weeks to assess progress. This plan represents a beginning point of help for Sam. The complexity of Sam's case suggests that there will be no easy solutions. Yet with school and community involvement, it is more likely that a comprehensive plan that reaches into all aspects of Sam's life will evolve.

Intervention Principle 5: Culturally Appropriate

There are different ways of communicating, relating, and interacting across different cultural groups. There have been findings with regard to specific mannerisms and behaviors, such as the physical distance that is considered appropriate in social interactions, voice tone, speaking volume, rapidity of speech, eye contact, linguistic variations, topics that provoke greater insult, posture, silence, and so on, that vary among cultures. For example, let's look at the distance between people in a social interaction. An aggressive individual will assume a position that is much closer in proximity to another person. Their physical closeness may be perceived as threatening and hostile. Yet it is important to maintain an awareness of differences and normative behavior across cultures in order to assess clearly whether the behavior is, in fact, aggressive. For example, findings have shown that Hispanics are more comfortable with less physical distance from others when contrasted with some other ethnic groups. Therefore, it is possible that one may misperceive a Hispanic student's physical closeness to another student as aggressive, whereas it may simply be culturally normative. Similarly, in Native American culture, it is valued to think and reflect before acting or speaking. Thus, confronting a Native American student about his or her behavior may result in a slower response than you as a teacher, counselor, or administrator may want or expect. You may interpret this response from your own cultural perspective as insolent and disrespectful. Paradoxically, the slowness of the response may mean the opposite for the Native American student, who may be carefully considering his or her response to you rather than making a hasty comment. Therefore, we must become familiar and respectful of cultural norms for different ethnic groups, while also becoming deeply sensitive to our own cultural underpinnings and biases. This awareness about ourselves and others becomes critically important when we are working across cultures, particularly with regard to aggressiveness, where responses, feelings, reactions, and consequences are heightened.

Intervention Principle 6: Interdependence

In the United States, we live in a society founded on rugged individualism. During the course of our history, we have come to value qualities such as individualism, independence, and self. Although these qualities have strong positive value, at times, they have contributed to a society where some individuals are inconsiderate of others, lack respect for the values and dignity of others and society, and simultaneously feel alienated from the world around them. A smaller percentage of those individuals who feel apathy, resentment, and anger toward others, family, and society resort to violence toward others and/or property. In some instances, the result of this is individuality without social consideration, concern, or respect that we see increasingly in our schools. Thus, it is our contention that a key element in addressing the escalation of violence in our society is to focus more on interdependence. Fostering better relationships, an understanding of others, and an ability to communicate more effectively and express one's feelings and needs all lead toward a reduction of violence. Consequently, we suggest that interdependence is an important guiding principle in diminishing aggression.

Group Work in Schools: New Directions

Group counseling is an important strategy for addressing underlying issues of respect and acceptance; alternatives to violence; consequences for behavior; and skills for academic, personal, interpersonal, and career success. In line with Intervention Principle 6, Interdependence, group work is an excellent intervention strategy for working with aggressive students. It is our belief that group work, in either the classroom or the counselor's office, would assist students to work through the emotional problems that promote violent behavior. The overall goal of such work is to move toward decreasing student violence and aggression. Having violence-prone youths acquire the skills and understanding necessary to develop more effective peer relationships, and having them work through the emotional problems that precipitate violent behavior, are two other important outcomes.

Groups could be led by the school counselor, school psychologist, and/or school social worker. Groups could also be cofacilitated by any of these professionals in cooperation with community-based professionals, such as mental health professionals from the local mental health clinic or counselors or psychologists specializing in working with children and adolescents. There could also be in-class groups in which the school counselor worked cooperatively with teachers to conduct sessions for the entire class. Group work in the classroom may be particularly helpful in addressing class climate and values.

It may be generalized to say that any student who exhibits violent behavior has multiple problems. Therefore, in groups that consist of at least some students who have been violent, the counseling emphasis should not be on aggression only, but should include the deeper spectrum of emotional issues. To emphasize anger management, peer mediation, or conflict resolution is helpful in that it provides cognitive and behavioral shifts and retraining that are important in addressing aggression. Yet the emphasis on only cognitive and behavioral interventions while neglecting affective issues is shortsighted and assumes that aggression stands by itself in the psychological domain of the student. Therefore, we recommend strongly that cognitive, behavioral, *and* affective fields be attended to in group work with violent students.

Cheryl, a 12-year-old, was angry and often verbally lashed out and physically hit her peers in school. The school counselor placed Cheryl in a counseling group for 10 weeks to provide her with an opportunity to talk about the things that made her feel so angry, explore the consequences of her behavior, and begin to problem solve how she might respond differently.

In putting together Cheryl's group, the school counselor considered a number of issues. How do students' strengths and weaknesses complement or detract from this group? Should these students be in the same group or dispersed into other, more varied groups? How many students should I include? Could the group get out of hand and become violent? How long should they meet? Is the group task focused, or is it more likely to be helpful as a process group?

The counselor finally decided to have five students, including Cheryl, in the group. All were having problems of varied degrees with self-control and aggression. Having students who can present diverse perspectives and model different problem-solving alternatives encourages a more constructive group process. Two of the students, similar to Cheryl, had difficulty managing their anger and, according to teacher reports, were getting worse. Two of the students in the group struggle with some of the same concerns as Cheryl and have made progress in communicating their frustrations in more positive ways. These students provided a strong modeling influence in the group.

We may be hesitant to work with the emotional problems of violent students, especially in group settings. In fact, we may even be fearful of encouraging a student to open up to feelings that are so powerful. We may be anxious that we are tapping into a place in the student that we are untrained to manage and that makes us anxious. Anyone who has observed the depth of pain and anger in a student who is violent knows it is profound. We may be scared that we cannot handle that place, that it is too much and, if touched, will be overwhelming. We may also be apprehensive that the student will get out of control as he or she touches those inner buried places that are so painful. Thus, supported by our professional training and methodology, we revert to the safer place of cognitive and behavioral interventions. This may cause us to worry about the student being out of control and our own fear about how we will manage. Again, the reversion back to cognitive and behavioral interventions. This anxiety about being able to control and manage students might even cause us to exclude a particular student for consideration as a group member. This may result in further isolation and prevent the student from experiencing the tremendous benefit that a group has to offer. Acting on these fears, we unconsciously perpetuate autonomy and individuality, rather than facilitate interdependence, which so many aggressive youth desperately need in order to be able to grow and change.

If we do overcome our consternation and place aggressive students in groups, what can we do to create effective, long-term change? Research has raised questions about sustaining cognitive behavioral intervention gains for aggressive youth. Peer mediation and conflict resolution may promote short-term change, assisting in the acquisition of new skills and techniques to manage anger, but long-term effects remain questionable. One of the most popular forms of school-based counseling for at-risk youths, the Student Assistance Program, has been criticized recently for lack of supporting data. This doesn't mean that you shouldn't implement these programs, but rather, carefully observe and see if these programs are truly working or are just the bandwagon for the moment. You may also want to consider integrating students at risk of violent and aggressive behavior with those who do not have these tendencies, or, as in Cheryl's group, with students who have made some progress in changing their behavior.

We suggest a different group approach to violent youth that focuses on the emotional problems that promote the aggressive behaviors. For example, the first author was consulting for a middle school. A group of the most violent youth was identified and encouraged by the school counselor to attend anger management group counseling with the consultant. In many schools, the aim of groups with this theme or similar themes is really to "control those kids (quickly)," but it misses the more important message for violent students: "How can we also help them heal so that they don't need to continue and escalate their violence?" Given the support of the administration to try an experiment and more deeply address the complex problems of these five youths, the group began by focusing on themes in their life that made them angry, rather than quick-fix remedies to control anger. They spoke about inattentive parents, bossy teachers, intrigue and fear about their exploration of sexuality, rejection by peers, lack of friends, and poor grades. As they explored these issues, the group simultaneously combined the teaching of coping strategies to handle these situations and techniques aimed at helping them reframe the situations where they became angry. The first three sessions in the group did not even mention anger or management strategies to contain anger; rather, they focused on the important inner worlds of the students. This was consistent with the two primary goals of the group that were parallel to cognitive and behavioral changes aimed at diminishing and eliminating violence. One goal was to give full attention to the pain and anger that was behind the students' aggressive behavior. It is the authors' belief that this must be addressed in order to introduce sustained and internalized skills and rethinking about their behavior. The second major goal was interdependence and social relationships. In the process of discussing and opening up for the first time about their deepest feelings, they also experienced what it was like to give and receive support from peers. This was a novel experience for all of the students. Each of the five students felt alienated and estranged from his or her peers and environment, which is a phenomenon that the authors have observed in multiple schools across the country with aggressive children. The ability to have a meaningful interaction with someone else was a profound experience in their healing and cannot be underestimated.

Thus, we would suggest that one of the paradoxes of group work with aggressive youth is not to focus on their violent behavior. Rather, addressing their deeply housed unmet needs, unshared feelings, and isolation within a group forum that is conducive to facilitating a sense of connectedness to others reduces violence and promotes a more comprehensive mental health.

Our recommendation here is that group counseling is considered an integral part of a larger network of interventions that includes programs within the community as well as the school.

Summary

Conducting business as usual will not work with aggressive students. This chapter presents guidelines that push beyond typical patterns of counselor-client interaction. We've suggested that school counselors step beyond the more traditional, content-based format for group counseling in schools to engage students in a more therapeutic group process that supports the surfacing and resolution of students' personal issues.

In the chapter that follows, we introduce a broadened role and program structure for the school counselor who is interested in developing a comprehensive violence prevention program.

5

Partnerships for Prevention

Students who are violent and aggressive have complex problems and needs. No single solution exists to help these students, nor can a single specialist or institution respond successfully to these needs by working alone. An effective, comprehensive violence prevention program requires schools, families, and communities to join together, both to help the single student who has already developed aggressive and violent behavior, and to plan broader based programs with a primary prevention focus. For example, let's take the case of Jason. He is a fourth-grade student at Parkview Elementary School. Jason lives in a public housing project just a few blocks from the school. Jason's parents are married, although Jason's father has recently moved out of the home. Jason's mother is currently employed, although she has a history of having a difficult time maintaining a job. Jason has two older siblings, both male and in high school. The neighborhood where Jason lives is plagued by drug dealers and prostitutes, as well as a large number of predominantly single-parent families who receive welfare or Social Security benefits. Because the drug dealing has escalated during the past few years, many members of the community fear for their safety and venture out only in the daylight hours.

Jason's teacher is worried that he might not be promoted to the next grade. He is failing or barely passing most of his subjects. Reading and math are particularly difficult. He rarely does his homework. Jason is belligerent to his teachers, gets into fights frequently in the schoolyard, and is disruptive during most classes. Jason's teacher referred him to the school's special education team for an evaluation, and as a result, Jason meets with the special education teacher for one period each day, and the reading specialist helps with reading. She also referred Jason to the school counselor, who has worked to help the teacher set up a behavior contract for use in the classroom. They have had little success in getting Jason motivated to participate. Jason's teacher speaks frequently by telephone with his mother about his behavior. Jason's mother seems reluctant to attend school conferences, although the school social worker was successful in getting the mother to attend the initial special education team meeting. Jason's mother was defensive at the meeting and expressed concern that Jason's teacher didn't like him. The school principal is considering a half-day schedule for Jason unless things improve soon. Unfortunately, Jason's fighting continues.

Sound familiar? In complex cases like this one, it is quite common for many professionals to be involved, each trying from his or her own perspective to help solve the problem. How "helpers" come together within the problem-solving process can have important implications for what you and others do. In this case, everyone involved functioned in isolation from each other with little communication or problem solving occurring between and across all participants. Although their intentions were to help the family, they only came together and communicated with each other initially through the special education team process, each assessing the problem, setting goals, and then drifting off to perform his or her helping function separately.

At another school, Henderson High School, a variety of programs exist to help students with complex needs. Julia, a 10th-grade student, speaks English as a second language and attends special ESOL sections of history and English. Two years ago, when she moved to the area, Julia was verbally and sometimes physically fighting with her peers, having regular confrontations with her teachers, and ignoring academic requirements and classroom activities. Now, as a result of a collaborative plan put together by a number of school- and community-based professionals in consultation with Julia's mother, Julia's academic performance has improved, fighting with her peers is significantly reduced, and she gets along much better with her teachers. She participates in a school-based counseling group co-led by a school counselor and a clinician from a local community mental health agency. This group targets minority students from high-risk neighborhoods and works to develop students' problem-solving skills, sense of self-esteem and self-respect, and ability to solve conflicts nonviolently. Julia recently joined another group led by another school counselor. This 5-week group emphasized study skills and academic achievement. Although she is still missing school sometimes, her school attendance has improved. Even better attendance is another objective. Other opportunities for Julia include peer mentoring, peer tutoring, and faculty mentoring. Julia's mother was recently referred to the Family Support Network, which links her to the school through a school-based, Spanish-speaking social worker. Through this network, Julia's mother can participate in an ongoing support group for Hispanic mothers and receive assistance in understanding the school system's expectations for Julia.

This scenario represents another occurrence common in many schools. Multiple services exist to help students and families. In some cases, the professionals who provide these services are employed by agencies under contract by the school system. In any given day, several different professionals may enter the school building, provide a service for a short period of time, and leave. In many instances, few mechanisms exist for integrating these service providers within the larger school structure. Often, this disconnect leads to a duplication of services and feelings of isolation on the part of the "visiting" service provider. Few opportunities exist for collaborative planning about cases or broader based prevention efforts. Fortunately, this disconnect among professionals and services does not occur at Julia's school. School and community service providers meet on a regular basis as part of a school-community mental health team to confer about cases, coordinate services, and plan joint programs.

It is the premise of this chapter that you, as a school counselor, teacher, or administrator, can play a crucial role in reducing school violence by participating, or even providing, leadership within your school for forming the type of collaborative, school-family-community partnerships needed to help students at risk of violent and aggressive behavior. Such partnerships are a natural extension of the teamwork you probably already perform.

In this chapter, we will focus on helping you develop the knowledge and skills that you will need to form collaborative partnerships to assist individual students and to create comprehensive, integrated-services prevention programs to reduce school violence. Specifically, we will discuss addressing the issue of aggression and violence in schools by examining what distinguishes collaboration from other types of interaction and by outlining procedures and skills for forming collaborative partnerships at your school.

Prevention Through Collaboration

Consultation is one of the primary functions of a school counselor, yet most counselors have received little formal training in models of consultation. When it has been included as part of a counselor's skill preparation, the training is often limited to consultation models that emphasize the counselor's role as an expert from whom others (parents and teachers) seek advice. The collaborative consultation model described here offers a new way of helping students who are violent or aggressive.

Through collaborative consultation, school counselors combine their expertise with the expertise of families, as well as others in the school and broader community, to create comprehensive solutions. The problem of violence is too complex for any professional or institution to work alone. By working as collaborative consultants, school counselors can provide leadership within their school to bring educators, families, neighborhood members, and community agency professionals together for joint problem solving. A collaborative consultation model does not presume that any one person has sufficient knowledge or information to develop and implement effectively a complete solution to the problem of violent and aggressive students. This means that you, the school counselor, need to function as part of a larger team. It is through the sharing of information among service providers and family members that a more comprehensive plan evolves. Within a collaborative consultation model, family members and professionals confer together as a team in order to identify student needs, strategize about how to help, implement interventions, and evaluate outcomes. In Julia's case, teachers, counselors, agency representatives, and Julia's mother conferred together and with Julia about how to help diminish her violent behavior.

It is a common practice when working with an aggressive or violent student for school counselors to consult with parents or teachers. In a typical, traditional consultation process, the parent or teacher depends on the counselor for advice about the problem and what to do to solve the problem. For some types of problems, this expert-dependent form of consultation is adequate. When dealing with the complexity of issues that generally surrounds students with violent behavior, however, this approach can be less effective. Let's take the case of Jamal. Jamal's mother recently contacted the school counselor for help with Jamal at home. His parents are at a loss as to how to manage his outbursts and defiance. They try to keep him in the house, but he refuses to stay in unless his father is at home. He hangs out with a rough crowd in his neighborhood, and his parents are very worried for his safety. They are also worried that Jamal might be getting involved with drugs. In approaching this problem as a more traditional consultant, the school counselor would listen, provide some strategies for the parents to try at home, and promise to meet with Jamal (if the school counselor had not already been seeing Jamal) to assess from Jamal's perspective what the problems seem to be. The school counselor and parents would agree to meet again to further refine what might be done to help.

The school counselor who functions from a more collaborative perspective will connect his or her specialized knowledge and expertise with the knowledge and expertise of other professionals and family members. Such helpers function interdependently—maintaining communication and contact with each other—throughout all phases of problem solving. In the case of Jamal, the school counselor would take some of the same initial steps as outlined previously. How the counselor interacts with Jamal's mother would be significantly different. When meeting with Jamal's mother, the school counselor would set a tone of collaboration by openly recognizing and valuing Jamal's mother's expertise about her son. Rather than providing advice to Jamal's mother, the collaborative counselor engages in an exchange that allows both parties to identify a common goal and next steps to achieving that goal. The process of establishing a mutually respectful and cooperative relationship becomes as important as the outcome. The counselor would also include at their next meeting (with the mother's permission) other professionals—teachers, school social worker, the school-based community mental health clinician, and the school's police department representative. At this meeting, a more comprehensive plan is developed to reduce Jamal's violent behavior and address associated problems. As you work more collaboratively, you will discover that the sharing of responsibility for outcomes and the ongoing communication and contact with other team members will help you feel less isolated, and often more empowered, to effect long-term change for your students.

Collaboration refers to how people interact as part of a team process. Schools at all levels have varied teams that come together to solve problems and plan new programs. People often think that as long as they sit at the same table to discuss a common problem or a student of mutual concern, they are collaborating. Not all teams, however, function collaboratively. For example, Sharon is the school counselor at a suburban high school that has been plagued with increasing incidents of violence, including afterschool vandalism. She has called together a team that includes someone from the local community police program, juvenile services, social services, mental health, and Big Brothers/Big Sisters, as well as several parents, to figure out a plan of action. She watches the group at their first meeting and sees that the mental health official is trying to take over the meeting; social services is blaming juvenile services for poor follow-up with some of the same students with whom they both work; and the police program representative is insisting on crafting the violence reduction program on police terms, which Big Brothers/ Big Sisters thinks is too authoritarian. "How will I ever get this group to authentically collaborate and communicate about the violence that is destroying our school and community?" Sharon wondered. "Ah," she thought, "I do remember some ways to do this." In fact, she remembered that collaboration has several distinctive features. As she remembered these concepts, it dawned on Sharon that she could share her expertise within the meeting by introducing these principles so that everyone could begin to work more cooperatively. So, as the meeting progressed, she started to lay out some of the guiding principles to the group.

"OK, we are coming in with differing opinions. I know that. But, let's focus for a moment. Collaboration is voluntary, right? When we all work together, everyone agrees to willingly cooperate by aiming toward the same goal? Right?" Sharon paused, waiting to see if everyone agreed. Then she continued, "You know, even in this place that I work, the school, I can't do anything with all of you, and you with me, unless we each choose to address this problem of violence together. I can't force you to work together, or work with me, but we all have to start out agreeing to tackle this problem together. What do you all think?" In her message, Sharon is pointing out that collaboration cannot be dictated, nor can members be coerced; rather, everyone has to agree to try to work together.

As the discussion continues, participants acknowledge their common concern about safety and the increasing violence. Some begin to question if things can really change. Some reflect on previous experiences with the school, where a lot of time was committed and no changes occurred. Sharon asks the school's principal to respond to these concerns. Remembering that collaboration requires parity among participants, Sharon reinforces that everyone is an equal participant who has an equal say in how decisions will be made. Collaboration cannot occur if one person (e.g., the principal) is perceived to have more power in the team's decision-making process.

The contributions of all team members, regardless of role or position (school counselor, community agency counselor, teacher, parent, nurse, principal, school psychologist, police representative), have equal value and weight in the decision-making process.

Knowing that a common goal is important in maintaining team members' attention to the problem, Sharon next tried to get all members of the group to agree on the common goal of working toward a safer school community. With this commitment in place, group members agreed to meet for a second time to identify strategies for accomplishing their goal.

At this subsequent meeting, Sharon reinforced that each member brings something unique to the problem-solving process. Sharon encouraged members to take responsibility for decisions and suggested that by the very nature of their shared participation, they are also equally responsible for whatever outcomes occur as a result of their prevention efforts. She playfully suggested they all either sink or swim together! Shared outcomes could mean change for individuals and families, as well as new programs and services. The creation of new service delivery structures—with team members representing different agencies and service providers—is itself a significant accomplishment.

As time passed, the group began to identify several prevention projects of interest. They began to strategize about how they will proceed and where they might find the resources to support their initiative. Things once again began to bog down as members shared some of their agency constraints on how money can be spent and services delivered. Sharon knew that for collaboration to succeed, everyone at the table needed to be able to share their resources—time, money, materials, and personnel—and that they would be the most successful in achieving their goal if resources could be shared with no strings attached. Sharon encouraged members to discuss their intended projects with their supervisors to determine the degree of flexibility that exists in applying agency resources. Group members also expressed interest in searching for grant possibilities that would aid their collaborative project.

Sharon also wanted to remember to point out that flexibility of role is an additional characteristic of a collaborative style of interaction. Team members recognize that no one person possesses sufficient expertise to single-handedly develop and implement a comprehensive solution to the problem of school violence. The integration of team members' multiple expertise strengthens the problem-solving process. In a collaborative model, team members work closely together and may even share aspects of each other's roles. For example, with Sharon's team, the police officer might work with the school counselor to implement support groups in the community for aggressive youth. The police officer might step outside of his traditional law enforcement role and acquire a teaching role in helping to train community mentors.

Making Connections

Forming school-community-family collaborative partnerships is an innovative process for reducing violence and aggression in schools. Collaborative partnerships view the entry of non-school-based personnel and family members into the school's program planning process as essential to the delivery of comprehensive, coordinated, and family- and community-sensitive services aimed at reducing aggressive incidents in schools. A shift from the more traditional system of service delivery in schools to a more integrated model requires you and others to make a substantial change in the existing school culture. A knowledge of student, family, and community needs; an understanding of the school as a system; and an already established role as a liaison to families and the broader community places the school counselor in a unique position to facilitate and encourage this shift. In a collaborative context, the focus of the school counselor's work as a consultant expands beyond change for the student, parent, or teacher to change for the school as a system and the school's procedures and structures for service delivery. This could mean that the school counselor spends less time working directly with aggressive students in a counseling capacity and more time consulting with family members, teachers, administrators, and school- and community-based service providers. The following sections further explore the counselor's collaborative consultant role by addressing the following:

- Potential partners
- How a school counselor might initiate collaborative partnerships
- What type of school-based mechanisms would be needed to provide ongoing support for collaboration

Potential Partners

Partners who work in the area of violence prevention and intervention may vary from one school to the next, or from community to community. Family members are essential partners, particularly when planning and managing individual services for a specific student with a problem of violence. In many families today, this may mean parents as well as grandparents, and could also include other extended family members such as aunts, uncles, stepparents, and cousins, or even legal guardians. Other partners we have found to be helpful include representatives from service institutions such as the departments of social services, health, and mental health; juvenile justice; and the police. Other important partners include representatives from helping institutions such as churches, parks and recreation, community centers, and libraries, as well as formal and informal neighborhood leaders.

It is important to spend time getting to know the broader community surrounding your school and the people who are respected within that community. Look for community strengths that might help in your efforts to suspend the increase in school violence; look for factors that might be contributing to the problem. Suggestions for how to get to know your community include the following:

- Learn which neighborhoods comprise your school community. Use a map to locate these neighborhoods. What areas are the most prone to violence? Drive through these neighborhoods and visit with community leaders. Observe the type of housing; the location of commercial areas; and the availability and accessibility of community services, including public transportation and churches.

- Find out if your school neighborhoods have community neighborhood associations, and meet with the leaders of those associations. These leaders might share your same concerns about the increase in violence. They may already have plans to help their neighborhoods stay safe.

- Investigate which services already exist to address the issue of aggression and violence. We have found that the police departments are often very active in communities and sponsor different types of prevention programs for children and families (tutoring, mentoring, field trips, athletic events). Church leaders can also be invaluable in helping you identify neighborhood leaders and projects.

- Conduct informal meetings at community locations in collaboration with other service providers. These meetings can be a useful way to begin assessing neighborhood needs and strengths. Community members who participate may provide perspectives on the problem that would have gone unnoticed from inside the school building. It wasn't until one of our first community meetings as part of a large-scale violence prevention initiative that we discovered how fearful people of all ages were of leaving their homes at night to attend social functions. Many feared being assaulted, and some feared having their homes broken into.

- Read local newspapers to find out about local issues and local businesses that might provide some working capital for violence prevention. Local media can also acquaint you with local leaders and people who are active in their communities. Sharon, the school counselor from our earlier example, invited Libby Pearce to join her school's team after reading about the work Libby did as a volunteer with aggressive youth at the elementary school in Sharon's school's catchment area.

Gaining Administrative Support

As anyone who works in schools knows, nothing changes in your school if your principal does not support the innovation. Gaining your principal's support is a critical first step in planning collaborative partnerships. Both authors have worked to initiate collaborative partnerships under the authority of a school system's superintendent. Even with the superintendent's mandate to reduce aggression and violence in the school through collaboration, we found that progress toward collaboration was slow in instances where the principal was not fully committed. One way we tackled this problem was to be clear about our mission, outlining clearly that we know that schools are in the business of educating young people and that academic success for all students is the major high priority. We tied in our violence reduction programs with academic achievement through collaborative partnerships in order to gain the principal's support. Aligning the goals of our partnership with school improvement goals and school district goals for violence prevention was a crucial strategy to employ full support.

Educating your principal about collaboration is also helpful. Principals have many things competing for their attention, and many may not really understand what makes a collaborative partnership important and distinct. Every principal wants a safe learning environment for his or her students. Broaden your principal's perspective of how collaborative partnerships can help reach this goal by sharing materials that you have collected. Information about other programs and projects that use a collaborative paradigm, such as James Comer's book *School Power*, and Lisbeth Schorr's book *Common Purpose: Strengthening Families and Neighborhoods to Rebuild America*, are two important resources. Because time is a factor, you might consider, as a starting point, preparing a short, one-page overview of the essential features of collaboration as a violence prevention strategy. This could also be shared with faculty.

Starting Small

Another important consideration when moving toward collaboration for violence prevention is to recognize that it is OK to start small. Rather than trying to engage all of the service providers and helping groups in your school community, you might begin by finding one or two partners who share your commitment to reducing violence. A large number of partners helps to ensure a more comprehensive program to address this very difficult problem. Yet taking small steps and joining initially with one or two partners can have its advantages. This is especially true if you are learning a new process at the same time that you are nurturing this process in others. Your work with parents and other family members can very easily take on a more collaborative nature through changes you make to your style of interaction. Later, as your confidence grows and your small successes increase in number, you can expand to a larger team.

Reaching Out to the Community

In moving toward building collaborative partnerships to tackle the problem of violence, it is important for you to redefine your role in the context of the broader community. This means that you will spend less time on activities focused solely within the school building and more time developing relationships and partnerships with service providers and community leaders in your school neighborhoods. This brings a new perspective on addressing violence, whereby your concern is no longer limited only to the school environment but to the total surroundings of the student. Learning about that community will take time and will require you to spend time outside of the school building, connecting with people and community resources. It is important to get to know not only the professionals to whom you might make referrals and the service providers who deliver services within your building and the nearby community, but also members of the neighborhoods that constitute your broader school community. It is particularly important to reach out to neighborhoods whose families are typically underrepresented in school groups like the PTA and at school events.

Finding a partner from these neighborhoods is critical to your ability to reach out to communities. Often, your potential partner is someone who works in the neighborhood, possibly with the housing authority, parks and recreation, library, or a community center. Mr. Hanson, an employee of a mid-sized city neighborhood boys' and girls' club, is an excellent example of the kind of neighborhood partner you need to find. Mr. Hanson lives in an inner-city neighborhood, where he both works and participates as a community representative on the local elementary school's integrated services case management team. Mr. Hanson is a vital liaison from the school to the families who live in his neighborhood. Families trust him, and knowing that he's at the school all the time, they often ask him to interpret information that comes home from the school. For example, parents who have questions about a student's report card frequently bring the cards to Mr. Hanson for an explanation. We can also find Mr. Hanson attending parent conferences at the school at the request of parents who might be uncomfortable approaching the school alone. Finding people like Mr. Hanson in your school community is an essential part of building collaborative partnerships. It has been our experience that even in the most impoverished, crime-infested neighborhoods, there are inevitably people like Mr. Hanson who are committed to building strong children and families, improving their neighborhoods, and reducing violence. Look closely and carefully—they are there, and you will find them. Such a partner can help educate you about the neighborhood culture and help connect you with others who are respected and valued by the community. These grassroots community people will be a significant help in ensuring a school-family-community partnership that reflects the composition of the broader school community. These partners will also provide important information about family needs, how to build trust, and, from a very practical perspective, how to contact families that may be hard to reach. Quite likely, these potential partners will also share your concerns about violence and your interest in violence prevention.

Reaching In to Faculty and Staff

Faculty and staff may be some of the more difficult people to move toward working collaboratively, especially when it comes to addressing aggression. Again, many schools already employ teams for a variety of purposes—student assistance, school support, educational management, pupil services, crisis management, special education admission/review, grade level, departments—although none of them is tied directly to the prevention of violence and aggression. Look again at the criteria mentioned earlier for collaboration. Many of the teams that are already operating in your school may claim to be collaborative yet function much more independently than interdependently. Asking people to change patterns of behavior is not always an easy task. Some are quite comfortable with the way things are and will never choose to work collaboratively. Again, starting small and moving slowly can be helpful here. Another useful strategy is helping people to see how working collaboratively toward violence prevention can benefit them.

Coming Together

After you have identified potential partners who have an interest in reducing violence in the school and community, it is important to bring these people together to formally initiate the partnership and begin program planning, either for individual students or for a broad-based school-community prevention program. Often, there is a sense of mistrust between families and schools, and agencies and schools. For example, teachers and other school personnel are often critical of child protective services for what they perceive as inaction; child protective service workers often complain that schools expect them to take action in situations where the law prohibits their intervention. In cases like this, mistrust could stem from misperceptions and inaccurate information. Building trust is an important task early in the life of the partnership. When your partnership includes representatives from varied service agencies, spend some time initially having participants learn about the services provided by each represented agency. Also, help members create a common vision of their work together—how would they like things to be—for a particular student, for their neighborhood, or for their school. Trust builds as the group experiences this common bond.

When organizing for a broad-based prevention program, we have found it helpful to begin the partnership with a team-building workshop held away from school to avoid interruptions and distractions.

We have enjoyed being able to work with teams for up to 3 days, and we have also worked in shorter, half-day formats. We used this concentrated time to identify common concerns and gaps in school- and community-based services, establish a common purpose for the partnership, and specify goals and objectives. This is also an important opportunity to introduce and reinforce collaborative group norms.

Mechanisms to Support Prevention Partnerships

A school-family-community mental health team provides a structure for bringing together school, family, and community representatives for joint program planning aimed at the prevention of violence and aggression. We use the term *mental health* in this context in its broadest sense. Strengthening children, families, and communities is the focus for the school-family-community mental health team. This team meets on a regular basis to

1. Identify school-family-community needs and strengths
2. Specify mutual goals
3. Develop a coordinated plan for services within the school, and between the school and the broader community
4. Initiate new programs
5. Oversee communication about services and programs to students, school staff, families, and community agencies and institutions
6. Make recommendations for change in school, agency, and governmental policies

This team would work very closely with the school improvement team to ensure that new program initiatives align with school goals. At River's Edge Elementary School, Gayle, the school counselor, participates on each team and acts as a liaison to the school improvement team from the mental health team. At first, having her join these teams was considered inefficient because doing so took her away from her other responsibilities. Her participation, consultation, and information from working closely with families, teachers, and administration now make her a vital part of the teams. Furthermore, she has been able to demonstrate how the work of the teams has affected educational performance and school climate by using information that she collects regarding attendance, suspensions, grades, proficiency tests, parental involvement, and referrals to the principal. The mental health team on which Gayle sits oversees program development. In some schools that are larger than Gayle's, the mental health team may have a subgroup that works primarily on program development, particularly around issues of violence and aggression. The mental health team's case management function provides an interdisciplinary approach to managing services for individual students at risk of violent and aggressive behavior. This team receives referrals from the school, parents, or agencies. The team reviews cases, develops an action plan for coordinated services, and monitors and evaluates progress.

An example may help to illustrate how this new type of team works. Shady Acres Elementary School provides many school-based programs for helping children succeed in school. Unfortunately, the school's efforts alone are not sufficient. Many of the students come from blue-collar neighborhoods with an increasing number of single mothers. The school also draws students from a local housing project. Many of the school's neighborhoods have a high crime rate; the use of drugs and incidents of violence are on the increase. To respond proactively to the violence and associated complex needs of many of the children at the school, Shady Acres Elementary initiated a collaborative, school-family-community mental health team—the CONNECT Team—to develop a plan for strengthening the families and community surrounding the school.

Participants on the CONNECT Team consist of representatives from the school (principal, school counselor, classroom teacher, special education teacher, two "anchor" parents who work as school-family liaisons, a grandparent, and a Headstart teacher); various community agencies (social services, police, parks and recreation); and community members interested in strengthening their neighborhoods by decreasing violence. The CONNECT Team's mission is to promote a healthy environment and to establish an atmosphere conducive to learning by engaging all segments of the community in a proactive effort. To this end, the team identified goals related to increasing parental involvement in the school and reducing community violence.

The team initiated two projects: the development of a school-based family resource center and the establishment of an integrated services case management team. A family resource planning group—consisting of the school counselor, the anchor parents, and a grandparent from the mental health team, as well as two additional parents, local members of the clergy, and a neighborhood civic group—met to develop a plan of action for the center, with an emphasis on decreasing violence. The principal, school counselor, school psychologist, school nurse, and community agency professionals from the mental health team took responsibility for forming the case management team. Both of these subgroups reported progress to the larger mental health team.

The family resource center was in full operation 9 months after the mental health team identified the center as a facility to play a pivotal role in primary prevention. The planning group met numerous times to develop procedures for the center and to determine services to be offered at the center. The school counselor helped the group develop a parent survey to assess family and community needs. Results guided decision making about the types of services to offer at the center. The Department of Social Services provided start-up funds to furnish the center, and the school provided space and personnel to help coordinate the center's activities. The school's anchor parents and the school counselor worked together to establish a volunteer network and to train volunteers in center procedures. Members of the case management team were able to use the center to see clients or hold meetings; often, this was a more convenient location for families than were agency offices.

The case management team discussed its first case 6 months after the team's inception. Team members spent the first 6 months establishing procedures for case referral and review, agreeing upon a clear mission to focus on aggression in the school, developing forms to document case work and action plans, and creating an interagency informed consent form. All procedures for this committee, particularly the informed consent form, needed to be approved by each member's agency.

A very important aspect of the success of the team is the shared case manager role by team members. Generally, the member who is most closely involved with the family at the initial point of contact assumes this role. Frequently, this person is the school counselor. Team members also share leadership of the meetings, but the school counselor prepares the meeting agenda and coordinates which cases are to be reviewed on certain dates, based on input from the members.

Not all service providers are involved with all families. After an initial case review, a smaller action group meets directly with the family to further identify needs and plan services. Although family members are invited to all meetings pertaining to their child, most attend the smaller, less intimidating group meetings. At Shady Acres, the school counselor coordinates the work of this smaller action group and, together with the anchor parents, encourages parental participation. The school counselor takes responsibility for monitoring school-based interventions and, at this point, may also provide counseling to the student and family.

Skills to Facilitate
Prevention Partnerships

There is no easy solution to the complex problems of violence and aggression. Collaboration between schools, families, and communities offers an attractive and viable possibility. Collaboration, however, takes time and requires significant changes in how schools organize and deliver services. This section highlights the skills that school counselors and other staff need to facilitate this paradigm shift.

For school counselors, all of the skills that you have acquired and use as part of your school counseling role are useful when forming and guiding collaborative partnerships to prevent violence, although administrators and teachers also may have had experience and training regarding interpersonal communication and teaching skills, which are also important in this arena. However, for school counselors, one of the primary areas of expertise that you bring to the team process to address these issues is your knowledge about basic counseling skills. The following summarizes the most important of these skills.

Communication Skills

The real value of creating multidimensional partnerships is the diversity of opinion rooted in the varied perspectives of school, family, and community representatives. Creating an atmosphere in which people feel comfortable expressing opinions and feel heard and understood is one of the challenges you will face as you bring this diverse group together. Effective listening enables group members to acquire important information and demonstrate value for the contributions of each team member. By using your basic listening skills (paraphrasing, reflection, clarification, open- and closed-ended questions, summarization, facial expressions, body posture, eye contact, and body movement), you will not only facilitate this important process, but also model effective skills for other members. It is important to remember that unlike many of the other collaborators, you have received training in these skills and thus have a special expertise to contribute.

Group Process Skills

One of the primary tasks for you as a school counselor or in other positions within the school, when working with collaborative teams, is to help facilitate the team process. Some things to consider when implementing this part of your role include the following:

Establishing a climate that conveys warmth and welcome to all members. Family members are often reluctant to come to school. Let's take the example of Stuart, who has been involved in two incidents of fighting with other children in school. His mother, Mrs. Cullins, was at the school last year but remembers how the counselor and principal talked down to her. "They were just rude and didn't treat me as if I knew anything." Sometimes, parents are hesitant to come to meetings because they have felt disrespected in the past. Mrs. Cullins also remembers her own school years. "They would just yell in your face or sometimes give you stupid punishments, even when it wasn't your fault. I couldn't stand it." These past memories make her wary to attend or trust the school officials who called her about Stuart. Then, Mrs. Cullins started to think again about last year. "When I was there last year, they had all of Stuart's teachers in the room telling me what he does wrong. No wonder he gets frustrated and lashes out when all they ever do is dwell on what's wrong with him. I know he's not perfect, but I don't think he's as bad as they make him out to be." Some parents who have immigrated to this country may also be confused about the school's expectations for students and how the school itself operates. For Mrs. Hernandez, coming to school is never a pleasant experience. She doesn't speak English very well and is embarrassed that her child is hitting other kids. She quietly thinks that the school blames her, yet she feels that she has little control over her child's school behavior.

It is not only the parents but also agency representatives who join the collaborative team who may be unfamiliar with the school and unsure of their role and the school's expectations. School counselors can provide an important bridge between the school, home, and community. The foundation for that bridge can be established during initial team meetings by making sure that all members are introduced, that all have an opportunity to speak, and that the group does not discount any member's contribution. Simple things like providing refreshments, introducing non-school-based team members to the office staff, letting people know where to put their coats, and facilitating the use of a telephone if needed are additional ways to say "welcome" and help people feel more comfortable as the group begins.

Establishing group norms to support collaboration. As the team begins to come together, it is important that the group be guided in establishing norms that respect and value each member. This is important in any situation, but particularly noteworthy when the group is dealing with volatile issues, such as violence, which elicit strong reactions in us. Some of the groups with whom we have worked have found these norms to be helpful:

▓ Be open and accepting of all questions.

▓ Use language familiar to all members; try to avoid using jargon.

▓ Speak up if confused. All questions are OK!

▓ Respect others' confidences by not sharing confidential information outside of the team.

Different teams will establish different norms. An important function for you as a team member is to recognize when a norm needs to be established and to raise this possibility with the group. In other words, ask the group, "Should we have a rule about inviting new members?" or "Does the group want to agree that in the future, the team member who presents the case takes responsibility for meeting with the family prior to the group's meeting? Also, if a parent will not be attending, should we agree that the team member also ask the parent to sign the written consent form?"

When working with administrators as team members, it is important to know if your administrator understands the collaborative paradigm and agrees to work collaboratively. Many administrators may think that they are acting collaboratively, yet they may be relying on a more autocratic style. This can put a school counselor or teacher in a sensitive position. It is important at the onset of the process to clarify and discuss thoroughly the features of a collaborative style and the benefits and difficulties of working within this paradigm. It is also a good idea to discuss early on with your principal the need for the group to reflect from time to time on its work together and to self-evaluate how well the members are collaborating. As an example, consider Derrick, a sixth-grade student who frustrated everyone at the school. He had a tough demeanor and argued with everything his teachers asked him to do. His mode of interacting seemed to say, "Yeah, make me if you can." Derrick has already been suspended during the first week in school for getting into a fight with another student. Derrick was up for discussion at the mental health team case management meeting. The school counselor suspected that the principal was as frustrated with Derrick as everyone else in the school. Before the case management meeting, the school counselor met with the principal to discuss Derrick's situation as well as how open the principal was to allowing team members to function autonomously and make decisions as a team. This proved to be helpful. The principal had some time to vent, and the school counselor had a better understanding of the limits of what the principal could and could not approve as action steps for Derrick. Asking your principal ahead of time how open he or she is to the collaborative process and what restrictions the team might have in light of school policies can save the team time and energy.

Empowering group members. You can empower members by encouraging and valuing their participation. To do this, be sure to provide opportunities for everyone to contribute. Be aware of silent participants, and ask them directly if they would like to comment. Reinforce all members' contributions. You might do this in several ways. Verbally acknowledging what the person has said by reflecting or paraphrasing provides immediate feedback and communicates that you heard the idea. Including a particular person's comments or ideas in written statements is also helpful. This is especially relevant when the group is generating ideas and these ideas are being recorded on the board or newsprint. An additional strategy for recognizing members' contributions is to bring ideas that get lost in the discussion back to the group's attention. Mrs. Lin had been invited to join the mental health team and has attended every meeting. She has been quiet, feeling somewhat embarrassed because her son was recently suspended for fighting. Mrs. Lin begins to tell the group about some of her worries about her son being out of control and how different he acts now that they have come to live in this country. The school counselor recognizes that this contribution is an important step for Mrs. Lin and the group. The counselor immediately restates what Mrs. Lin has said, thanks her for her contribution, and asks her to tell the group more about her concerns.

Managing dominant members. This is probably one of the more delicate tasks for someone facilitating a group's process, especially when dealing with volatile issues such as aggression, where people have strong feelings. On one hand, you want to encourage all members' participation, yet at the same time, you need to guard against a few people trying to control the process and, in some cases, inhibiting others from participating. This alone could suggest a power differential, thereby making it more difficult to establish a feeling of equality among members. Once again, because we are dealing with aggression that is closely tied to power issues, we must be particularly sensitive to how we address this within our own teams. When you notice someone being aggressive in the group by trying to dominate, several strategies might prove helpful. You may recognize what the person has said by restating or paraphrasing, and then redirecting the discussion back to the group by asking a question. For example, you might say, "Ms. Jones seems to think that having parents hired as classroom assistants would be helpful when the three students in the back of the room start threatening the other students. Can some other group members comment about this idea?" or "Can anyone else think of some other possibilities?" Another possibility is to reflect on your discomfort with the group process and share with the group your observation of how hard it seems for everyone to get a chance to share. You might ask if anyone else in the group feels similarly. You might then help the group decide how to handle similar situations in the future. Another example of how someone might dominate is the situation presented by Ms. Javitz. Ms. Javitz, a high school teacher, had a recent confrontation with a student, and it left her very upset. The student was angry about a discipline referral that Ms. Javitz made, and after school, this student followed Ms. Javitz to her car. Although the student said nothing, his nonverbal behavior left Ms. Javitz feeling threatened. Unless the student actually did something, the principal said that she could take no action. Ms. Javitz was using the team meeting to vent about this incident. The school counselor in this case reflected tactfully how this experience underscored the reason that this team was formed and then invited Ms. Javitz to meet with her privately to discuss the issue at greater length.

Providing leadership. To discuss leadership in the context of collaboration might appear to be contradictory. Leadership implies authority, which seems incompatible with parity, one of the distinguishing features of collaboration. Yet different group members bring different areas of expertise to the group, and thus, in their own way, each provides leadership to the group. Group process skills are a significant area of expertise for the school counselor and others when working with teams to reduce violence. When you facilitate a group's process, you assume a leadership role within that group. In the spirit of collaboration, the leadership of group meetings may be shared or rotated depending upon the group's task at the moment and levels of competence and skill for group members.

Facilitating decision making. Partners will have to make many decisions related to services and programs to address violence, including individual students and broader based prevention programs. Members will also make decisions about how to allocate limited resources. This could be a source of conflict. Partners frequently come to the partnership wanting to know "what's in this for me (my agency, family, etc.)." You can facilitate the team's decision-making process and mediate conflicts by

1. Ensuring that the group hears all members' ideas
2. Helping the group members think about whether or not the choices they make move them closer to, or further from, their shared goals
3. Helping the group make choices based on an evaluation of possible consequences and other, more direct, costs and benefits

Problem-Solving Skills

Counselors are very proficient at helping clients solve problems. The same skills you use in a counseling context are useful when working with groups focused on finding solutions to violence and aggression in schools. Generally, we think of six steps when implementing a problem-solving process. Given your problem-solving expertise, guiding the team through this process may be an important team role for you to assume. Because most of you are already familiar with these steps, we will not elaborate on them here but rather name the step and offer some words of caution based on our experiences working with groups on problem solving with an aim at decreasing violence.

Step 1: Identify the problem. This is a critical first step and one that many groups want to skip over quickly so that they can get on to solutions. Be careful about moving too fast through this process. Having a clear understanding of the problem and agreement about the problem helps to define what changes are needed. When working with groups to plan school-community change efforts as part of a broad-based prevention program to reduce violence, assessing community needs becomes an important part of problem identification. Community empowerment for change is tied directly to members of the community feeling that the plan for change responds to their needs. The collaborative process begins with this step and the exchange of information between school, family, and community.

Step 2: Establish goals. This is probably the hardest part of problem solving. Participants can often articulate what they want, yet this becomes stated in vague, general terms. "We should all work together to reduce violence" is a worthy goal, but it is general enough so that there is no clarity about how to approach and succeed at accomplishing this objective. Your job is to help the group specify what it wants in language that is concrete and measurable in order to reduce violence in the school. When establishing goals, it is also important that the group be realistic about the expected outcomes. When Mr. Frank suggested the elimination of all acts of aggression and violence as a goal for the group, the school counselor acknowledged his contribution and asked the group to reflect on how realistic it would be to expect the elimination of all such actions. Solving complex problems is neither easy nor accomplished in a short time. Having short-term goals, and long-term goals with clear benchmarks for success, will help team members feel that progress is being made. Mr. Frank's team wanted to diminish aggressive behavior, but it also recognized the need to increase students' positive interactions and use of socially acceptable coping skills.

Step 3: Generate strategies. Participants will have many ideas about how to create a safe school and community environment. Allow plenty of time for brainstorming and for the ideas to percolate. Groups tend to get critical of ideas during the brainstorming process.

We encourage you to help the team members to get all of their ideas out on the table, and only then begin to assess the feasibility of each suggestion. Mrs. Steers, from the largest city high school, learned that she must be very patient and help everyone speak out about their ideas, no matter how farfetched they seemed. Allowing the team members to not limit themselves by traditional obstacles during brainstorming fostered creativity and new ways of thinking about violence. Mrs. Steers realized this, even though she was aware that she could quickly think of numerous obstacles to many of the suggestions, as well as ways to implement the projects that were proposed. Mrs. Steers shared with her principal how facilitating the team to decrease violence in the school had taught her valuable lessons about patience, "breaking out of the box" to be creative, and the spirit of cooperation.

Step 4: Develop an action plan. An action plan identifies next steps and describes roles and responsibilities for the different participants on the team. If the team is collaborating around the needs of a single student or family, the plan will focus on the concrete steps necessary to help these individuals. If the team is collaborating around broader based school and/or community needs, the plan will probably be more complex and could have several phases. You might even find it helpful at this point to have subcommittees responsible for developing certain aspects of the overall plan, because violence is multi-faceted and complex. Subcommittees could meet separately and then report back to the larger group. It is important to remember in this step the complexity of the problem we are tackling—violence is multifaceted, with many associated issues.

Step 5: Implement the plan. Team members who work together in trying to implement strategies for change work more collaboratively than do teams whose members function in isolation from each other. Traditionally, community agencies, schools, and businesses may meet occasionally yet, for all practical purposes, remain separated and isolated from each other. Team members who put aside these boundaries more openly share knowledge, skills, and resources; interchange roles; and share functions during implementation, resulting in more comprehensive and better plans to work on reducing violence.

Step 6: Evaluate outcomes. We suggest to you that evaluation is critical for any project that reduces aggression in the school. We want to know if our plan has worked and if it has any correlation to the overarching academic goals for the school, such as proficiency tests, academic performance, suspensions, and attendance. Conducting the evaluation comes after implementing the plan for change. Most groups forget to think about evaluation until it is time to assess outcomes. Planning for the evaluation, however, needs to take place earlier. How will this group know if violence is diminished? How will this group know if students are having more positive inter-actions with peers and teachers? How will we know if grades have been affected or absenteeism reduced? We have found it useful to have the group plan for the evaluation at the same time that it is establishing goals and developing an action plan. This helps to ensure consistency between our goals and what we are evaluating, and it also ensures that the measurability of the team's goals and the plan that they develop to achieve those goals are realistic. It is also important to develop a plan for monitoring progress while imple-menting the plan for change. It is important to use the results of your evaluation to assess progress toward goals so that you can determine if the project or program that was developed is, in fact, effective. If the evaluation fails to denote progress—if violence and aggression have not diminished—help the group determine why not, and revise the action plan as needed. Possible reasons to consider are goals that are unrealistic, plans that were improperly executed, inadequate strategies, and insufficient methods of evaluation. School personnel should be cautious here and should not become too attached or personalize the plans as theirs regardless of results. This will only lead to rigidity and turf issues with other individuals and agencies.

Skills for System Change

This chapter implies that the organization of mental health ser-vices in schools today is not as efficient or effective as it might be to help students and schools reduce violence. The current procedures and processes for service delivery warrant change and require new organizational procedures; new mechanisms for service delivery;

and new partnerships between schools, families, and communities. Direct service alone is insufficient. Individuals who behave aggressively or violently warrant a continuum of services, from direct (one-to-one counseling) to indirect (educational programs, consultation with teachers and parents, family therapy), and from intervention to prevention. Furthermore, change for the individual cannot happen in isolation but must occur within the context of the multiple systems that surround the individual. This would suggest that both the individual and the systems (school, classroom, family, peer group, neighborhood) surrounding the individual could become targets for change. As school counselors and other educational staff begin to redefine their position in light of collaboration and service integration, the reality of being an agent for systemic change is an important, emerging role.

How can you as a school counselor, teacher, or administrator influence systemic change to lead toward safer and less violent schools? Awareness of several basic systemic principles is an important first step. These include the following:

1. *The whole system is greater than the sum of its parts.* The school and the community in which you live exert influence on you and everyone else in a unique way. When the members of your school or community are together, their collective behavior may be very different from how each of you acts outside of the system. How many times have you worked with a student in your office and gotten an impression of a cooperative and reserved student based on your relationship? Then, to your amazement, you later encounter the same student in a classroom context or with a group of peers and find the student's demeanor and behavior to be much more aggressive. To get a more complete picture of an individual, the school counselor, teacher, or administrator operating from a systemic perspective should observe and seek information about a student's behavior in a variety of contexts.

2. *Change in one part of your school or linked community affects all of the other parts.* This ripple effect suggests that change in some element of your school will ultimately force adjustments or change in other parts. You and other individuals within the school are living and

moving within the larger system of the school, which has a life of its own. Furthermore, you are interdependent on the school, so that what you and your colleagues do affects the school system, and what happens in the larger system affects you. The result of this is that changes that you choose or are forced to make individually can occur as a result of change in the larger school, or changes that you make can affect the larger system. How a school chooses to respond to an increase in violent and aggressive student behavior could represent a good example of this principle. For example, when faced with an increase in violent acts (individual behaviors), the school changes school security measures (systemic change) and initiates violence prevention programs (systemic change), including working with the police and neighborhood leaders to establish a neighborhood-based peer mediation program (systemic change). The goal of these systemic changes is a decrease in episodes of individual violence and aggression. In addressing the problems of violence in your school, it is important to know the interplay of dynamics as you move ahead with strategies and programs to improve school safety.

3. *The school or community system as a whole is more powerful than the individuals working within the system.* When you or any other individual attempts to change, the school may hinder your or your colleagues' ability to change. There is an innate tendency to maintain the status quo, because your school or school-agency collaborative partnerships have momentum to maintain homeostasis. You have probably seen this principle in action; Ben provides a good example. Ben hangs out with a tough group of kids. Although he seems to want to change his image as a school troublemaker, the minute he gets back with his friends, he's up to his old ways. Ben seems to know what to do differently to reach his goal, but making the actual change in his behavior has proven to be more difficult. Ben feels secure with his old friends, and he's not ready to explore other socializing options.

Frequently, schools provide multiple services to students with complex needs and try hard within the school environment to help the student make changes in behaviors, attitudes, and values. Frustration sets in, however, when the systems outside of school (family, neighborhood, peer group) fail to support the school's efforts and, in some cases, work against what the school is attempting to do. This is well illustrated by Ben's case, when the teachers, principal, school counselor, and juvenile services agency caseworker became disillusioned with Ben's failure to change. The staff grew impatient and resentful of Ben, which caused him to become more alienated and reluctant to participate and agree to their interventions. As his aggressive and antisocial behavior escalated, agency personnel and school staff began to argue, tensions heightened, and their efforts for cooperation were at risk.

School counselors, teachers, and administrators who work with students at risk for violent and aggressive behavior would do well to realize that change for an individual student is closely connected to major changes in the student's world. Work directed at changing the teachers' or parents' behavior, the organization of the classroom, the family structure, or the neighborhood or peer culture will effect a more lasting change for the student. When working to effect broad-based systemic change, however, school personnel must keep in mind that collaboration with other service providers is essential.

Detecting problems in a school and having the school be responsive to recommendations for change can exist as two opposite ends of a continuum. You will find that not all schools are open to change or responsive to your feedback and recommendations, even if they are completely reasonable and make sense to you and others involved. Resistance to change occurs frequently and should be expected. Remember that the principle of homeostasis—the school's or community's effort to maintain the status quo—is quite powerful. Yet when stress or tension occurs within these environments, or between the school and the larger suprasytem that includes community, businesses, school district, and so on, the school may be motivated to change. Ironically, violent and aggressive behaviors are stressors that do motivate schools to change. These changes are frequently motivated by a school administrator who recognizes that "business as usual" is an insufficient response for accomplishing goals aimed at safe schools and diminished violence.

Again, it is important to keep in mind the maxim of starting small. It is unrealistic to think that a principal would welcome unsolicited recommendations for how to change his or her leadership style, or how the school might restructure its case management process. The same would apply to teachers who might need assistance with making changes in classroom organization and structure, or to families. When working from a system-focused perspective, you need to do important groundwork before moving to action. Establishing a trusting relationship with members of the school and community systems and helping them recognize that a problem exists are important first steps. Helping a school recognize and appreciate its strengths is also important. School counselors, teachers, and principals will also find a collaborative approach to systemic change to be more effective than functioning as a solitary expert.

Summary

School counselors who want to effect long-term change in behavior for violent and aggressive students need to appreciate the possibilities as well as the limitations of direct service models of intervention. Effective problem solving for students with complex needs sometimes requires schools, family members, and community groups to work together in new ways. This chapter suggests that you as a school counselor, as well as other school personnel, can provide leadership within your school for forming collaborative partnerships and facilitating the systemic changes necessary to maintain such relationships. The shift from a more fragmented way of doing business to a more collaborative service delivery model challenges school counselors to rethink their roles and functions. When working within a collaborative paradigm, the indirect services of consultation and coordination assume a more primary position than does direct, one-to-one counseling. Some new skills and knowledge are necessary for school counselors to acquire as they move toward collaboration. This chapter described some of these changes. The chapter also suggested that the school counselor's existing repertoire of skills is important and useful in his or her collaborative consultant role. School counselors have a history of adapting their position to meet changes in social conditions. We are confident that once again, school counselors will successfully meet this new challenge and exciting opportunity.

On to Chapter 6 and a closer look at ourselves as potential problems in the intervention process with violent and aggressive students. Counselor, look within!

Additional Reading Sources

Comer, J. (1995). *School power.* New York: Free Press.

Friend, M., & Cook, L. (1996). *Interactions: Collaboration skills for school professionals* (2nd ed.). White Plains, NY: Longman.

Keys, S., & Bemak, F. (1997). School-family-community–linked services: A school counseling role for changing times. *The School Counselor, 44,* 255-263.

Lerner, R. M. (1995). *America's youth in crisis: Challenges and opportunities for programs and policies.* Thousand Oaks, CA: Sage.

Schorr, L. (1997). *Common purpose: Strengthening families and neighborhoods to rebuild America.* New York: Doubleday.

6

Avoiding
Professional Pitfalls

Knowing Our Own
Childhood and Adolescence

Working with violent and aggressive youth is one of the most difficult things one can do professionally. It typically causes us to react
strongly, with our emotions manifesting in many possible ways. We
may become very angry with an aggressive child for making us feel
out of control or scared. We may feel sad, remembering other incidents or events that we have experienced or observed. We may even
want to go and hide, and try to avoid the angry and painful feelings
that emerge as we are faced with a youth's fury, hurt, or rage. Yet it
is essential that you know and understand the origin of these reactions in order to work effectively with violent youth.

Our response to these dramatic incidents is based on our own past experiences. Growing up, everyone faces moments when there is strong anger and physical and emotional aggression in his or her life. Our first contact with these feelings is during childhood, either within our own families, in schools or the community with peers, or with our peers' families. Regardless of where we first have contact with violent behavior, it makes a strong impression on us and begins to define the way we will respond to aggressive situations for the rest of our lives.

For us to be effective in working with aggressive students, we must be fully aware of what happened to us during our early years of childhood and adolescence. For example, Randy is a school counselor who is well known for his sensitivity and warmth with students. Even though Randy appears very centered and able to help with the problems that students regularly bring to him, there is a sense by teachers and students that when there is a potentially volatile situation, Randy is ineffective. Several students and a teacher once saw him fall apart when two ninth graders with whom he worked started yelling and physically threatening each other. Randy started to breathe rapidly; his voice was shaky; and he backed away from the two students, saying in an uncharacteristically meek voice, "Please stop, please stop." In a personal discussion with a friend who was a teacher in the same building, Randy shared that "I am afraid when people get really angry. I don't really know why, maybe it has something to do with when I was younger."

If we followed up on this comment by Randy and explored more closely what he meant by this, we would find out that Randy grew up in a home with an alcoholic father who regularly verbally and physically abused his mother and sister. Although Randy had tried to stand up to his father at a younger age, he quickly learned that he was too small to stop his father's wrath and abusive behavior. Randy remembered that his challenges only exacerbated his father's anger. He finally resorted to hiding in his room behind the bed, hoping that the fury of the moment wouldn't spill into his bedroom on that particular night. The result of this experience has made an otherwise seemingly well-adjusted Randy fearful of any conflict, especially if people are angry or threatening.

Although not all of you have had experiences as traumatic as Randy's, we have all experienced strong reactions to someone's anger when we were younger. It is this awareness and insight into our own background that we must understand in order to work through these issues. In our opinion, it is only after we resolve these past experiences that we can be effective working with aggressive students.

Nonjudgmental, Really?
A Roadblock in Disguise

Early in our professional training to learn how to work with children in schools, we are taught that we should be neutral in our response to students. We are trained to focus on students' learning and the higher goals to which our classrooms and schools aspire. As counselors, we are taught to be nonjudgmental, accepting the person as a person rather than evaluating him or her as good or bad, worthy or unworthy. Even though this is one of the most difficult personal and professional traits to master, many of us do succeed in gaining some degree of neutrality in our responses to the wide array of issues, problems, and concerns that accompany children.

Yet in our experience, the very angry and violent student challenges us at another level of openness and judgment-free responses. This is the child whose serious problems and aggressive behavior touch in us our earliest experiences with conflicted relationships, many of them still unresolved in adulthood. The violent child moves us toward reactions that are rooted in our most primitive emotional states, causing anger and/or fear that accompanies our anxiety as we face our responsibility in handling a potentially dangerous situation. Simultaneously, these strong reactions cause us to feel, think, and behave in certain ways as we respond to the violence. Part of the difficulty here is that it also challenges our first line of neutrality, testing what we believe is true about who we are.

What presents the greatest problem at this moment of being tested is integrating the value system that we think we hold to be true and the strong emotional reaction that we have to violence. In that situation, do we still maintain neutrality? Are we still viewing the violent student as someone who is in tremendous pain and needs attention, clear limits, caring, and help to maintain control? Or are our strong feelings and reactions to that child or adolescent causing us to have strong opinions about that aggressive student, judging him or her to be a "bad kid," an "unreachable child," or even someone who "shouldn't be allowed to come to this school."

These responses bring us back to our very core, our own childhood and earlier experiences. Yet the problem is that these reactions do not help aggressive students and contradict the very heart of our training and attempts at value-free professionalism. Therefore, we suggest that all professionals carefully and honestly examine their own beliefs and values, and understand that you do have them. Our inability to recognize them is a large impediment to actually attaining an authentic nonjudgmental perspective in our work.

Self-Disclosure: Toward What End?

Frequently, professors in counseling are asked by graduate students in training, "How much should I self-disclose to clients/students with whom I work?" They want to know if it is OK to talk about their personal relationships, their children, past wild behaviors, drinking or drug use history, sexual experiences, abuse, and so on. This question is fairly straightforward, and we have given the same answer for decades: When sharing about yourself isn't motivated by personal needs and is designed to be helpful to your clients/students in their growth and development, then it is appropriate to share feelings, stories, history, thoughts, and so on. When you are self-disclosing to meet your own needs (e.g., you want to be liked, to be seen as cool, to be needed, to be appreciated, or to be seen as important), then it is inappropriate.

This answer becomes more complicated when working with aggressive children and adolescents in schools. A primary reason for this is that students who are aggressive need clear and well-defined boundaries. The key words here are "clear" and "well-defined." When dealing with potential violence, it is important that there is no confusion about the limits to creating safety. One aspect of setting boundaries is to form and establish a clear definition of our role in helping the violent child to gain self-control. Therefore, to reveal aspects of our personal life to a child who needs clear parameters about who we are in relationship to them may serve only to create more bewilderment and confusion. This would be especially true when we are first getting to know an aggressive child and are uncertain about each other. The relationship boundaries at this time are very unclear. Therefore, until an alliance with the student is clarified, it is important to maintain perceptible limits as we better define our connection with the student. Attempts to join by self-disclosing at this stage may create more difficulty for a student who is feeling out of control. Over time, as the basis for the relationship is better understood, you may find yourself revealing more personal information, but initially, it is important to be more reserved when working with an aggressive child.

Modeling

As counselors, teachers, or administrators in schools, we carry tremendous power. Our influence is sometimes far beyond our awareness. You may have been surprised when a student from 5, 10, 15, or sometimes even 20 years ago has come back to you with accolades about something you did or said to him or her. This also holds true for aggressive students, who are carefully watching how we behave, the way we handle certain situations, what we do when someone is testing us, and how we talk to our peers and administrators. This was brought home to the first author a number of years ago when he was the director of a mental health treatment program for "untreatable" (the word used in those days) adolescents, many of whom were highly aggressive. The program included an extensive clinical component, residential treatment, and an independently accredited school. It was interesting to observe the adolescents as they became healthier and adopted the behavior of educators, clinicians, administrators, and residential staff. As a staff, we could almost identify our own mannerisms in the young people as they moved on the road to psychological health. Our work, of course, was to move them beyond this starting point of modeling our behavior and to help them find their own styles that would fit in better with their emerging new identities. The striking part of this was the continued recognition by the staff about the power of our positions in relationship to the youth. The same holds true for you as school staff, especially as you are working with youth who have problems, such as aggressive students, who must take many steps in their growth. It is crucial that we maintain a sensitivity about the influence we have on violent youth, especially when they are in a phase of growing and changing.

Self-Tapes

When working with a violent child or adolescent, we have suggested earlier in this book that you must maintain contact with not only the acting-out student but also the world around him or her. We have encouraged you to observe yourself. One important question to ask yourself is, "What am I doing and why?" This question and self-reflection may almost be described as a running inner tape, whereby we are monitoring our own reactions and responses. This inner dialogue with ourselves may be important in helping us determine our reactions to the immediate moment and assist us in responding more appropriately.

You may ask, "How can I ever do that? I'm in the middle of a highly charged situation, a kid is about to explode, and I am supposed to talk to myself?" These are fair and good questions. The answer is that the result of doing this may shape our interventions much more effectively. But doing it, like anything else, takes time. To begin to have this inner voice that has the potential to provide insight and guidance in the moment, one must begin by trying it out. Experiment with it; see how it may guide you. And practice; like developing other skills, you must run your self-tape when you are speaking with a potentially violent student and try it out. At first, it is awkward and maybe even distracting. Over time, it will become easier, until finally, it is second nature.

Debriefing: A Critical Task

Violence is highly emotionally charged. As we have discussed, there are strong reactions, memories from developmental years, flashbacks, and lingering charged emotions. In the middle of this, we are expected to be consummate professionals—centered, involved, caring, effective, and then "back to the job." We suggest that in order to continue to work effectively with aggressive children, debriefing is necessary.

In our rapidly moving schools and society, we forget to take care of ourselves. Working with violent students is one of the most trying, if not the most taxing, aspects of the job in a school. Much too often, the message after an incident is, "OK, get back to class." Yet everyone, students and staff alike, are talking about the incident and can't really think of much else.

It is our recommendation that after any violent incident, allot time to process the experience on two levels. First, process with students who have been directly affected by what happened. We may forget that students may become highly troubled by observing violence. A recent study by the first author found that youth who observed traumatic experiences had more mental health problems than did those who actually experienced the trauma. Sometimes, we are afraid of the power of what students are feeling, and we try to bury and forget the incident. Other times, it has just been too painful for us, so that we don't want to go back and relive the incident with students, particularly if we haven't processed what happened ourselves. It is imperative that students have assistance in understanding what they have witnessed or heard about, and that they are supported in making sense of it. Their self-understanding and processing of violence is essential in aiding them to get back on task in the classroom or school activity. It is also essential for you and your colleagues to debrief. Even you, as a staff member, have a reaction to violence. Furthermore, you may not only have witnessed an incident, but also had the responsibility to manage the situation, which may cause you to be shaken up. It cannot be emphasized enough how important it is for you and other staff to process violent events with peers on both an informal and a formal basis. This is contradictory to the norm in some schools, whereby the directive is to "Move on, we have work to do." Debriefing decreases built-up feelings of frustration, anger, or resentment and, subsequently, burnout.

Buying Into Chaotic Systems:
Joining the Problem

There are healthy and unhealthy school environments. Dependent upon the environment in which you work, there are different responses to aggressive students. You may wholeheartedly agree with some practices, whereas other policies, procedures, or attitudes may seem too harsh, unfair, or even harmful to students. The first author met recently with key principals in a large urban district to discuss how to better reach the difficult students, many of whom were aggressive. One principal, with a student body of 250 students who were earmarked as college bound, earnestly commented, "Out of my 250 students, 50 are thugs. If I could get all of them out, then I would have a good school!" Through further investigation, the first author found that the policies and practices in his school reflected that philosophy, with an unspoken intention to remove as many of those 50 "thugs" as he could.

Not all schools are as blatantly discriminating about their problem students. Typically, these attitudes are more muted and subtle. Yet variations of these values and subsequent practices exist throughout the United States. The problem also becomes yours if a punitive approach is taken that never gets to the deeper underlying issues promoting aggression, rather than addressing violence in a deeper, more circumspect way. This places you, if you see the world differently, in a very precarious position, between good practices for troubled students and bad policy.

We encourage you to constructively challenge bad practices and policies. Knowledge about the underlying causes of violence, ways to respond to the problem, associated issues, and staff reactions to violence would place you in a position of responsibility to address larger system responses. To bring your knowledge forward and challenge bad or misguided practices is important in redirecting and redefining the macro view of the issue. We believe that if you do not contribute to reducing violence in a constructive and positive manner, then you, too, are part of the problem.

A Final Thought

Preventing violence and aggression in your school community is a pressing task. Although most of you will be, and have been, spared the stress and overwhelming anxiety of having to respond to a traumatic, violent crisis, many of you confront on a daily basis students who are angry, volatile, and sometimes dangerous. Schools today are very different places from their predecessors of 10 or even 5 years ago. In our work with school counselors, we are continuously impressed with the dedication and hard work that we witness over and over again as counselors create hope in students who had no hope and, in general, make a difference in the quality of life within their buildings. We hope that what we have offered within these pages are ideas, skills, and strategies to add to your existing repertoire of talent and ideas. The types of students that we describe within these pages are some of the most challenging youths with whom you will ever be asked to work. Yet you and countless school counselors like you, as well as other school staff, step forward and meet the challenges that these students present again and again. Unfortunately, as counselor educators, we are not able to send you forth from our doors equipped with all that you will need to know—hence, learning on the job is critical. It is our hope that the stories in these pages and the suggestions from our experience and the experience of other counselors will enrich your on-the-job experience. We wish you much success as you move forward to new levels of professional service.

Index

CORWIN
PRESS

The Corwin Press logo—a raven striding across an open book—represents the happy union of courage and learning. We are a professional-level publisher of books and journals for K–12 educators, and we are committed to creating and providing resources that embody these qualities. Corwin's motto is "Success for All Learners."